A Survey of World Cultures

Asia and the Middle East

Jane W. Smith
Carol Sullivan

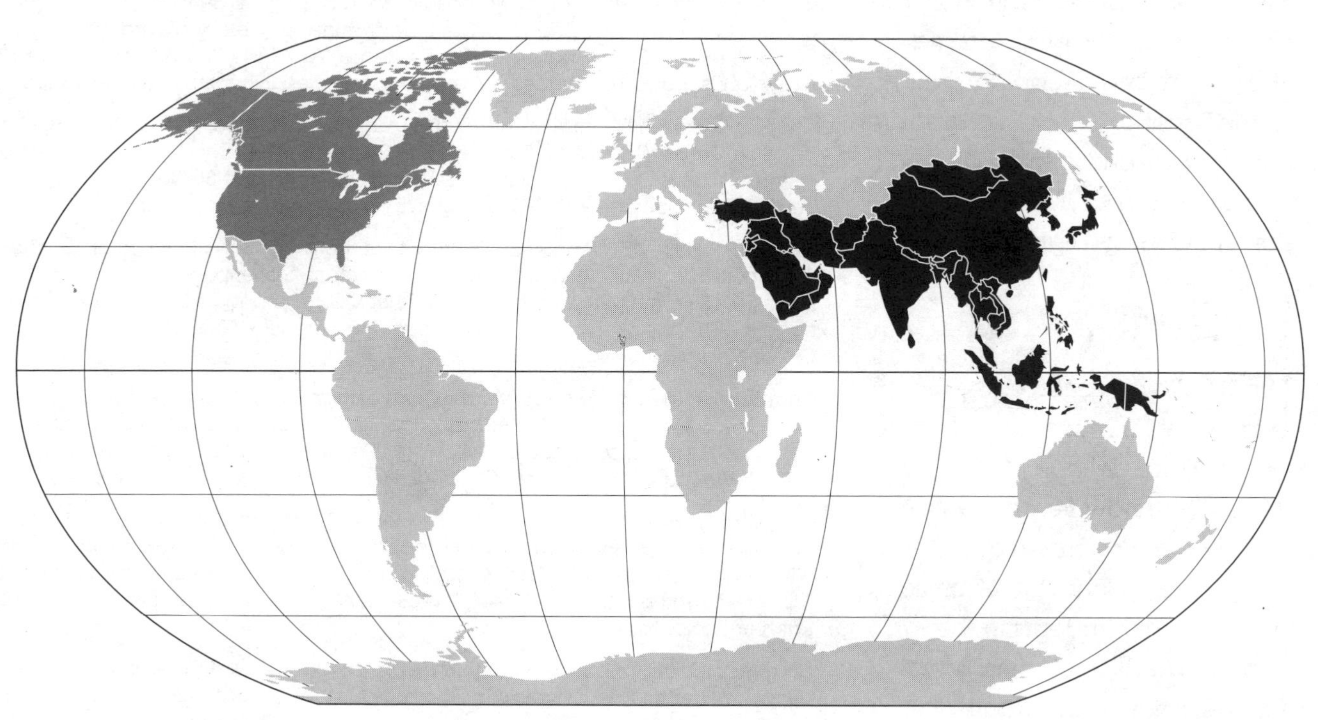

AGS®

A SURVEY OF WORLD CULTURES

ASIA AND THE MIDDLE EAST

Jane W. Smith

Jane W. Smith received her Master of Arts in Teaching as a reading specialist from Emory University in Atlanta, Georgia. She taught basic reading skills at the Schenck School in Atlanta. She now teaches remedial English and reading skills at Forsyth County High School.

Carol Sullivan

Carol Sullivan received her Bachelor of Science degree from Jersey State College of New Jersey. She now teaches secondary Special Education at Forsyth County High School in Georgia and instructs students in the content areas, including social studies, science and math.

Special thanks to Marcel Lewinski for his description of a visit with a Japanese family.

Photo Credits

Cover Photographs: Upper left: M. Bernheim/Woodfin Camp & Assoc.; upper right: L. Hebberd, Woodfin/Camp & Assoc.; lower left: G. Ludwig, Woodfin Camp & Assoc.; lower right: SuperStock

Chapter 1: Page 2, Michael S. Yamashita/Corbis; page 4, Bettman/Corbis; page 7, Charles Gupton/Stone; page 9, Mike Blank/Stone; 10, Pete Seaward/Stone; page 13, Kevin R. Morris/Corbis; page 16, Koji Sasahara/AP/Wide World Photos; page 17, AFP/Corbis; page 18, Charles Gupton/Stone; page 20, SuperStock International

Chapter 2: Page 25, Carl Purcell/Corbis; page 27, Art Directors & TRIP Photo Library; page 28, Janet Wishnetsky/Corbis; page 29, Reuters NewMedia Inc./Corbis; page 32, Bettman/Corbis; 33, Art Directors & TRIP Photo Library; page 35, SuperStock International; page 38, Art Directors & TRIP Photo Library

Chapter 3: Page 43, Dennis Cox/ChinaStock; page 45, SuperStock International; page 46, SuperStock; International; 50, Alain Le Garmeur/Stone; page 54, Yann Layma/Stone; page 55, R. Belbin/Art Directors & TRIP Photo Library; page 56, Julia Waterlow/Corbis; page 59,Christopher Liu/ChinaStock; page 60 Keren Su/China Span; page 64, Dennis Cox/ChinaStock

Chapter 4: Page 68, Kevin R. Morris/Corbis; page 69, H. Rogers/Art Directors & TRIP Photo Library; page 72, AFP/Corbis; page 75, SuperStock International; page 77, Kevin R.Morris/Corbis; page 78, Michael S. Yamashita/Corbis; page 81, Reuters NewMedia Inc./Corbis; page 82, Chuck Fisherman/PictureQuest (PNI)

Chapter 5: Page 90, Nigel Dickerson/Stone; 94, Margaret Gowan/Stone; 95, Jex David Cole/Corbis; page 96, Andrew Errington/Stone; page 97, Owen Fraken/PictureQuest (PNI); page 100, Kevin R.Morris/Corbis; page 102, SuperStock International; page 104, Jack Fields/Corbis; page 105, Galen Rowell/Corbis; page 106, Wolfgang Kaehler/Wolfgang Kaehler Photography

Chapter 6: Page 110, SuperStock International; page 114, John and Lisa Merrill/Stone; page 118, Reuters NewMedia Inc./Corbis; page 121, Lois J. Barnes; page 122, H. Rogers/Art Directors & TRIP Photo Library; page 123, H. Rogers/Art Directors & TRIP Photo Library; page 125, Dennis Cox/ChinaStock; page 127, SuperStock International

Chapter 7: Page 136, Paul Chesley/Stone; page 142, Christine Osborne/Corbis; page 150, Michel Lipchitz/AP/Wide World Photos; page 151, Christine Osborne/Christine Osborne Pictures/MEP; page 153, Art Directors & TRIP Photo Library; page 155, Lorne Resnick/Stone; page156, David Turnley/Corbis

ISBN: 0-7854-2625-6

Product No. 90930

Contents

Contents

Chapter 3: China

Chapter 4: Taiwan

Chapter 5: Southeast Asia

Contents

Asia and the Middle East

Introduction

Introduction

What Is Culture?

People all over the world have the same basic needs. But they meet these needs in different ways. They learn their ways of thinking and acting—**traditions**—from their ancestors. These traditions are known as culture.

Culture is the way people live. Culture is what people believe. It is how a group of people behaves with one another, and how they behave with people outside their group. Culture is what makes every group of people special and unique.

Culture is made up of many different things. Culture is the language, music, and art of a people, and the holidays they celebrate. It is their **economic** system and the ways they are governed. It is the ways they dress and the products they produce. It is the customs, religions, and inventions that a group of people shares.

Humans have lived on Earth for a very long time. During this time, the ways people live have changed. Humans have learned to adapt and use their environment to survive. The climate and the kinds of food that were available have given people certain choices. They have figured out what to use for clothing and shelter to keep themselves warm and dry, and what to eat to make themselves strong and healthy. Most importantly, humans have learned to communicate. This process of adapting to the environment and learning how to communicate marked the beginning of culture.

Why We Need to Understand Culture

Understanding a nation's culture isn't easy. But we need to know something about cultures around the world for at least three reasons.

First, studying culture helps us to understand ourselves better. Studying culture helps us to understand why we act and live the ways we do.

Second, understanding culture helps us to more effectively deal with change.We understand things like how people might feel about new inventions and discoveries that will affect their lives.

Third, understanding culture helps us to work better with people of other nations and cultures.We understand that we may see things very differently from each other. Knowing this helps us to work together for a better future.

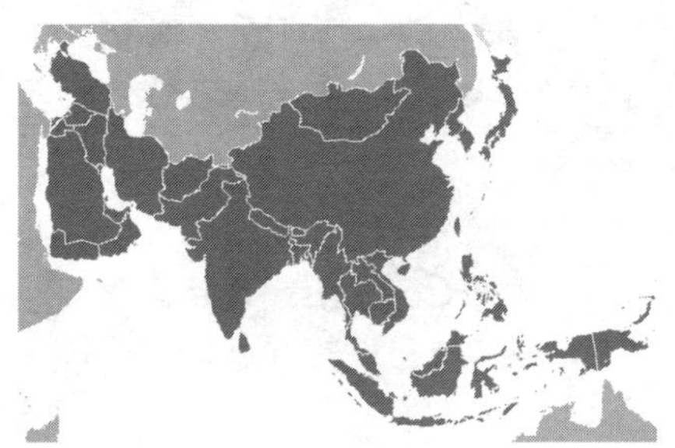

Words to Know

economy:
the system of making and trading things

tradition:
something that has been handed down by generations that came before

Learning About Culture in This Text

Asia is located east of Europe. It is separated from Europe by an imaginary line from the Ural Mountains to the Caspian Sea and then through the Black Sea. Asia and Africa are divided by the Suez Canal. The Pacific Ocean forms the eastern border of Asia. Australia, an island continent, is to the south. Asia is so large that its northern border touches the Arctic Circle. The Middle East is the region of Asia where Asia, Africa, and Europe meet. It is mostly desert, with some mountains. One area that is not desert, and receives adequate rainfall, is the Fertile Crescent. This V-shaped plain is formed by two rivers, the Tigris and the Euphrates.

In this text you will be looking at the cultures of the many people who live in Asia and the Middle East. You'll learn about their religions, languages, family life, ways of earning money, recreation, art, music, and other things. You will discover what physical features such as mountains, deserts, plateaus, lowlands, and islands are found in Asia and the Middle East. These physical features greatly affect the way these people live.

For example, most of the Middle East is desert. The people here live in areas where there is a natural water supply, such as the ocean, or the Fertile Crescent, which is formed by two rivers. Southeast Asia has more than 300 million acres of hardwood trees. The people here work in the forestry business. The small island country of Japan is one of the world's industrial leaders, but compared with other countries such as the United States, it does not have much room for farming.

Compass rose

Learning about Maps and Globes

You need to know the meaning of some terms to understand maps. A *map* is a picture of the earth, or part of the earth, on a flat piece of paper. A *sphere* is a round body, or a ball. A *globe* is a round ball that stands for the earth. A *hemisphere* is half of this globe.

Maps and globes can show different things. There are many different kinds of maps. For example, a *physical map* shows such things as mountains, rivers, and plains. A *political map* shows borders between states or countries. A *climate map* shows hot, cold, dry, and wet areas. A *natural resources* map shows things like the locations of minerals and oil. Maps and globes can also help you understand the relationships among these things. All of these things influence culture.

The *equator* is an imaginary line around the middle of the earth. It separates the earth into the *Northern Hemisphere* (above the equator) and the *Southern Hemisphere* (below the equator).

Introduction

A *legend* on a map will explain the meaning of any symbols on the map. It may also have a measure that is equal to a certain number of miles. That way, you can find out how far apart the locations on a map really are.

Lines of *latitude* are imaginary lines running east and west (across) on a map. These lines measure, by degrees, the distance north or south of the equator. A *degree* is a unit of measure. The equator is zero degrees. One degree of latitude is approximately 69 miles. So, places along the 10 degrees north parallel line are 690 miles from the equator. Latitude lines are sometimes called *parallels* because they are the same distance apart from each other, no matter where they are located.

Lines of *longitude* are also imaginary lines drawn on a map. They run north and south (up and down). They measure the distance east or west of the *prime meridian* (see below). These lines of longitude, called *meridians*, are the same distance apart at the equator. However, they are not parallels because they do not stay the same distance apart. If you move from the equator to the North Pole or the South Pole, the distance around the globe gets smaller. The distance between lines of longitude decreases as you move away from the equator. All of the lines of longitude come together at each of the poles.

The *prime meridian* is a line that runs around the world from the North Pole to the South Pole. It goes through Greenwich, England. It is located at the zero degree meridian. It separates the earth into the Eastern Hemisphere and the Western Hemisphere.

A *compass rose* like the one shown here can be found on many maps. It shows which way north is located and may show other major *directions* as well. Remember that north is a direction. Usually, but not always, it is placed at the top of a page.

In this book, you will see a small map in the lower right-hand corner of every right-hand page. This map shows Asia and the Middle East. As you move through the book, the country you're studying will appear black on that map.

Each chapter in this book begins with a Map Skills exercise. This exercise will introduce you to the country you will study in the chapter. It will also give you a chance to become more familiar with the terms you've read about in this introduction.

Studying the maps in this book will help you to learn about the cultures of Asia and the Middle East.

REVIEW

Answer the following questions.

1. What is the difference between a globe and a map?
2. What is the equator? How does it divide the globe?
3. What is the prime meridian? How does it divide the globe?
4. In what direction do latitude lines run?
5. How do latitude lines measure distance from the equator?
6. In what direction do longitude lines run?
7. How do longitude lines measure distance from the prime meridian?
8. What is a hemisphere?

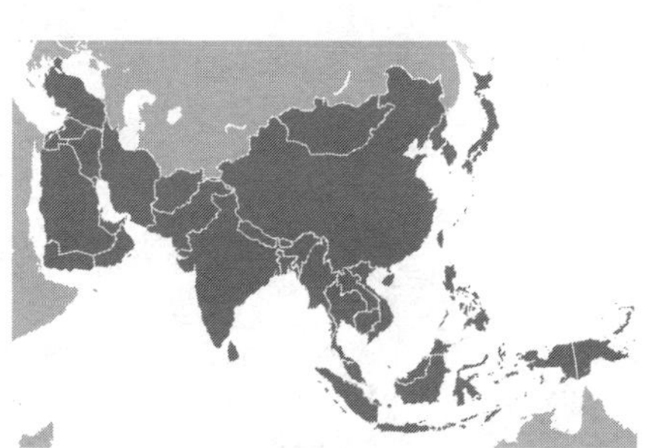

JAPAN
CHAPTER 1

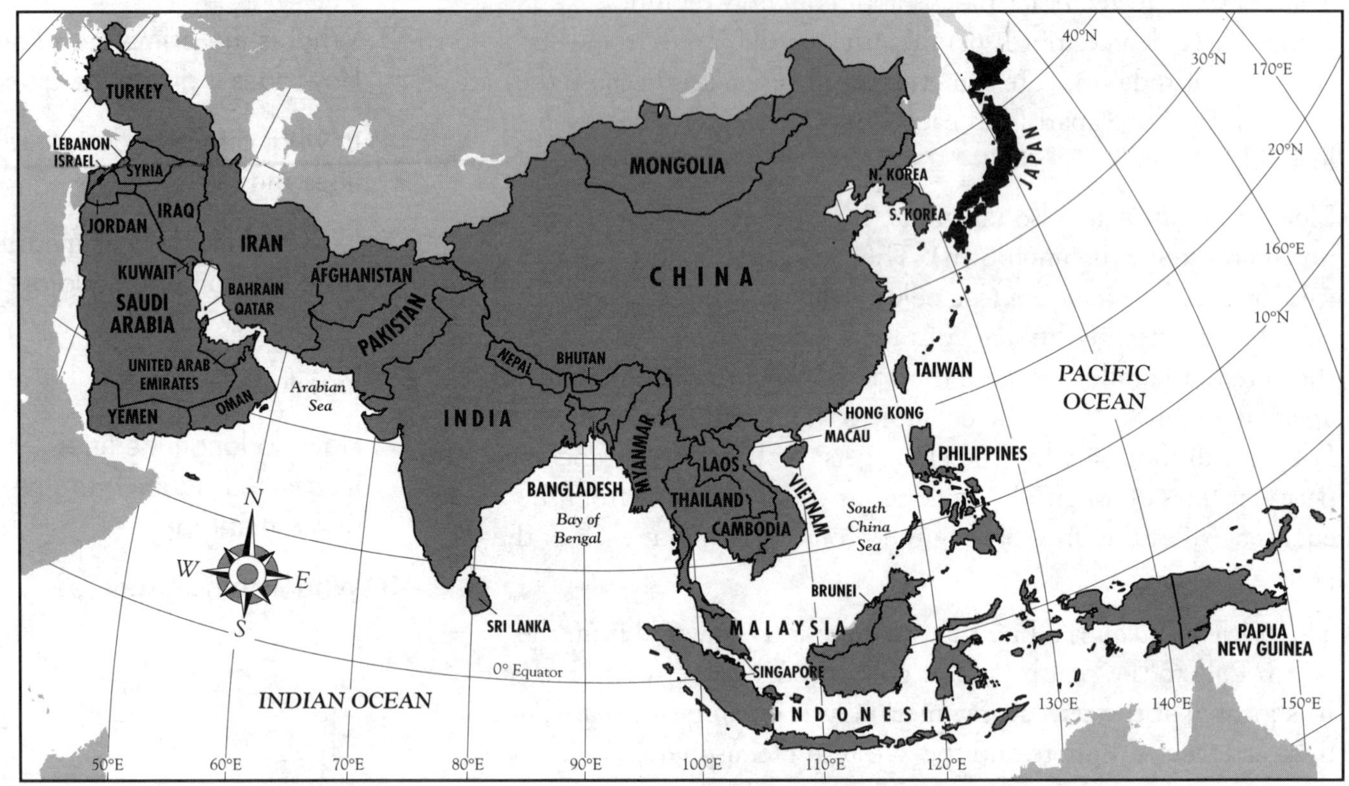

Fast Facts

- **Japan is made up of four main islands and thousands of smaller islands.**
- **A 33-mile-long underwater tunnel connects two of these islands.**
- **Japan is one of the world's largest producers of cars and electrical equipment.**
- **Samurai were brave, loyal soldiers in ancient times.**

Chapter 1 – Japan

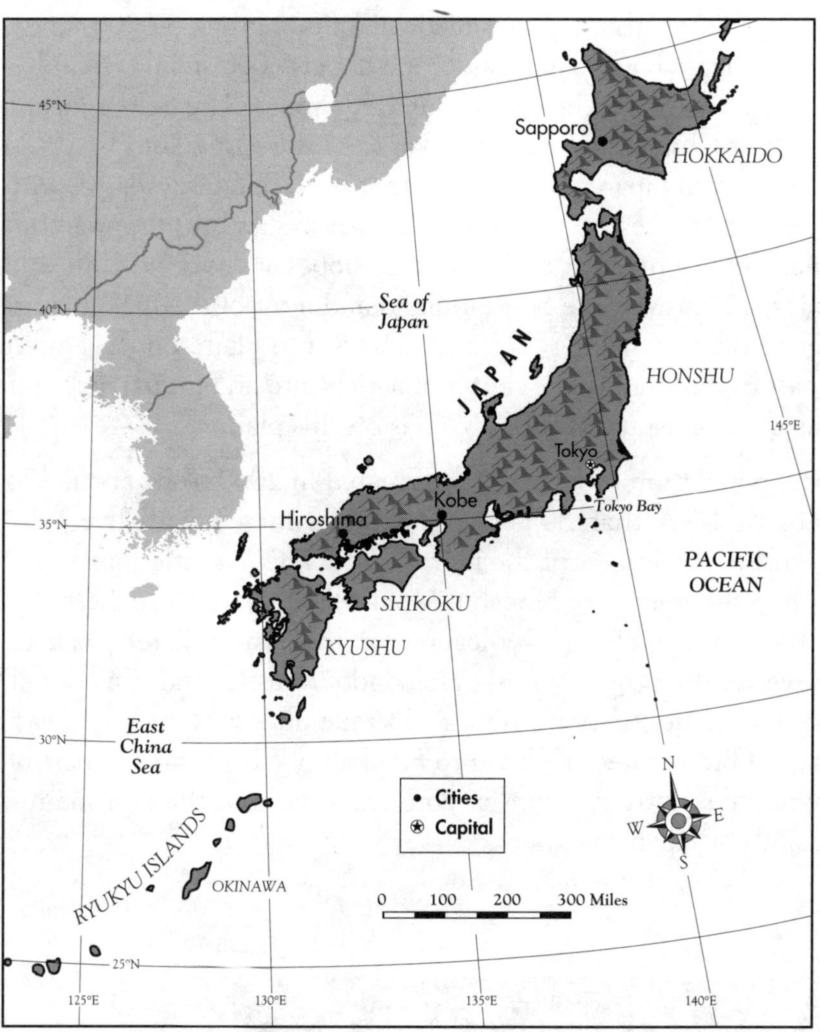

MAP SKILLS

Japan

Directions: Study the map above to answer these questions.

1. What is the approximate distance from the northern tip of Hokkaido to the southernmost tip of Okinawa?
2. If you traveled from Sapporo to Tokyo, in which direction would you be going?
3. About how far is it from Hiroshima to Kobe?
4. In which direction is the equator from Japan?
5. What natural land feature covers most of Japan?
6. Between what lines of latitude does most of Honshu lie?

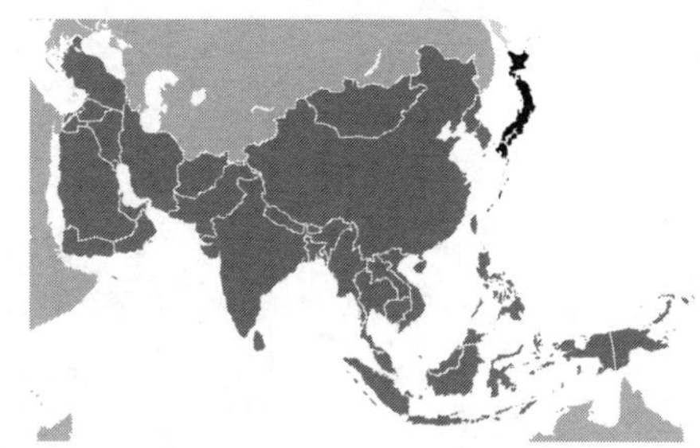

Chapter 1 – Japan

Words to Know

industry:
a branch of business or manufacturing

LESSON 1: A Journey Through Japan

Did you know that Japan is made up of more than 3,000 islands? That's right! Four main islands and about 3,000 smaller islands stretch in a curved line for about 1,500 miles. The Sea of Japan and the East China Sea separate Japan from the east coast of Asia. On your visit to Japan, you will find that it is a mountainous country of great natural beauty with high snowy peaks and rushing waterfalls. Many of the hillsides and mountain slopes are covered with thick forests. However, the best farmland and most of the big cities are found on plains along the coast. The Kanto Plain, on the eastern coast of Honshu, is the center of agriculture and **industry** for all of Japan. The capital city of Tokyo is on this plain.

The population of Japan was estimated in 2000 to be about 126 million. More than 80 percent of the Japanese people live on Honshu, the largest of the four islands. The majestic Japanese Alps rise in the middle of Honshu. Mount Fuji is Japan's highest mountain in a chain of volcanoes on this island. Later you can travel to the other islands—Hokkaido, Kyushu, and Shikoku. These are all smaller than Honshu. A 33-mile underwater tunnel was built in 1988 to connect Honshu to Hokkaido. This tunnel is part of a national railway system that conveniently links the four main islands of Japan together.

A national railway system links the four main islands of Japan.

Japan Has Four Seasons

Northernmost Hokkaido and the middle island, Honshu, have cold winters and warm summers. The southern islands of Kyushu and Shikoku have hot summers and mild winters, like the state of Florida. Rain is plentiful in most of Japan. Monsoons bring cold air to northern Japan in winter and warm air to southern Japan in summer. Typhoons are a problem, and several strike the country every summer or early fall. The strong winds and heavy rains of these violent storms can destroy crops and houses.

LESSON REVIEW

Directions: Number your paper from 1 to 5. Then answer the following questions.

1. What bodies of water separate Japan from the rest of Asia?
2. What connects the four main islands of Japan?
3. Why is Japan considered a country of great beauty?
4. Compare the climate of Japan with the climate of the United States. What is one difference between the two climates?
5. Would you like to visit Japan? Give two reasons for your answer.

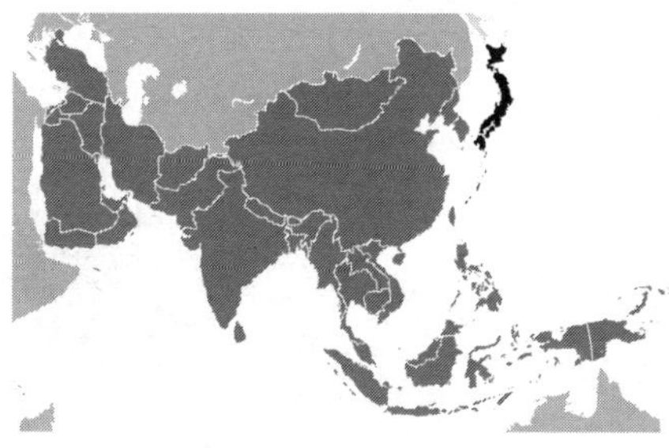

LESSON 2: Changes Through the Years

Words to Know

export: to send goods to a foreign country

merchant: a person who buys and sells goods

minister: someone acting for someone else

minority: less than half of the whole part

retaliate: to pay back or get revenge

People who hunted, fished, and gathered plants lived on the islands of Japan as long as 6,500 years ago. Some scientists believe that Japan's earliest inhabitants were a group called the Ainu from the island of Hokkaido. Today the Ainu make up Japan's largest **minority** group.

Early Rulers of Japan

Originally, Japan was ruled in a way that was copied from the Chinese. There were provinces and villages just like in China. The Japanese also borrowed their system of writing and calculating, along with their calendar and ways of telling time, from the Chinese.

In the late eighth century, Heian, now the city of Kyoto, became Japan's capital. A strong royal family, the Fujiwaras, took control and ruled Japan for almost 300 years. The heads of other powerful families were called daimyos. Yorimoto was head of one of these families. He was given the name *shogun*, which means "general." The shoguns ruled Japan until 1867, when the Tokugawa shogun came into power. The first emperor after Tokugawa's rule was Emperor Mutsuhito in what was called the Meiji period.

The Rule of the Tokugawa Family

Definite social classes existed during the rule of the Tokugawa shoguns. The highest class was the *samurai*, which means "one who serves." These warriors received land from a lord and fought for him.

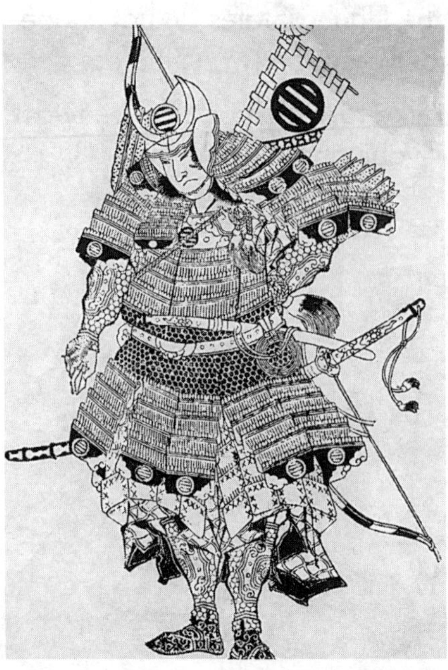

The samurai were fearless soldiers, but they were also artists.

Peasants, who produced food for the nation, came next on the social scale. Then came the craftsmen who made their goods from materials produced by others. Socially, the lowest class was the **merchants**. The craftsmen and the merchants had to live in areas away from the higher social classes.

Beginning of Modern Japan

The Meiji period marked the beginning of modern Japan. Instead of the samurai, the new emperor and his advisors established a navy and army. He set up a system of education that required school for all citizens. Railroads and telegraph systems improved communication. Modern methods of banking and taxation were created. Americans and Europeans advised Japan's industrial leaders. Out of this came the *zaibatsu*, the large corporations owned by single families. Some names, like Mitsubishi, are familiar today. Many Japanese resented the zaibatsu because of their great power.

A constitution was written stating that the emperor should be the head of state and that he shared command of the army and the navy. He could appoint **ministers** to assist him. The constitution also called for a two-part parliament called the Diet.

Unsettled times followed. Japan fought a war with China. This war was fought because both countries wanted to control land and trade in Korea. The Koreans rebelled against Chinese control in their country. Both China and Japan sent troops there to stop the rebellion. It was stopped, but neither China nor Japan would leave. They both wanted to rule Korea.The Japanese claimed victory and won the island of Formosa (now Taiwan) and some land in China. France, Germany, and Russia interfered and made Japan return the land to China. Because of differences concerning Korea and Manchuria, Japan declared war on Russia in 1904. The treaty that ended the conflict declared that Korea would become a colony of Japan.

World War II and Japan

World War II began in Europe in 1939. Because Japan wanted to control all of eastern Asia, its relationship with America became strained. The United States stopped **exporting** goods to Japan. On December 7, 1941, the Japanese surprised the United States with an attack on its military base in Pearl Harbor, Hawaii. America **retaliated**, and fierce battles in the Pacific followed.

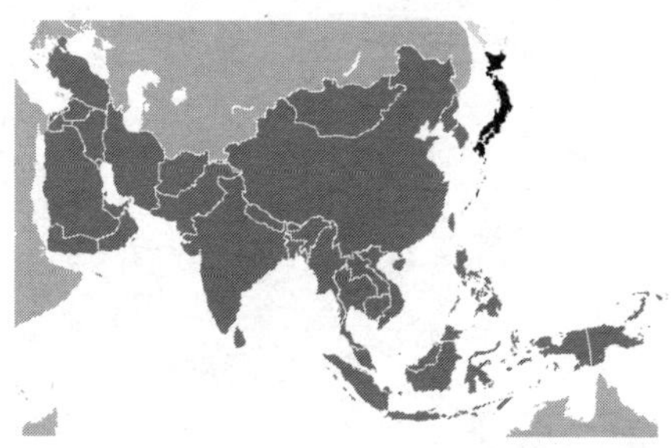

Words to Know

ally:
a person or a country who has a common plan or goal with another person or country

technology:
the use of science to do practical things

The United States ended the war by dropping atomic bombs on the Japanese cities of Hiroshima and Nagasaki. This was the first time that atomic bombs were ever used against human beings. No one could predict the horrible results of this action. Thousands were killed instantly, and thousands more died as a result of the bomb. Those who survived were severely burned and scarred for life.

After World War II

Japan was in ruins. Its economy was totally destroyed. After surrendering, the government of Japan was taken over by the Allies under the leadership of General Douglas MacArthur. The purpose of the presence of **allied** troops was to end the strong military in Japan and to set up a democratic government.

Economic changes took place during the occupation. The zaibatsu businesses were split up. Labor unions were formed to represent the needs of the workers. Landowners were required to sell most of their land. The released land was then divided among the peasants.

Within 10 years after the end of World War II, the Japanese—with American help—made great economic gains. They used Western **technology** for producing products that they sold worldwide.

LESSON REVIEW

Directions: Number your paper from 1 to 5. Then answer the following questions.

1. Who was Yorimoto?
2. What were some changes that took place during the Meiji period in Japan?
3. What were two changes that took place during the allied occupation of Japan?
4. Was the occupation successful? Explain your answer.
5. Do you think that the U. S. should have bombed Japan to end the war? Explain your answer.

LESSON 3: Western Influence on Japan

A visit to Japan reveals that life there is greatly influenced by Western countries, especially the United States. Baseball is the most popular sport. The people wear the same type of clothing that is worn in the United States. A popular American fast-food chain has built more than 2,800 restaurants in Japan.

Today, Japan is a modern, industrial nation with a low unemployment rate. As a result, the standard of living in Japan is very good. People can spend money on recreation and entertainment activities. Movies, plays, concerts, traveling, and sightseeing are enjoyed by the Japanese. Like Americans, they buy many electronic goods and appliances.

However, the Japanese have not given up their own culture. The kimono is still worn by many people during festivals and holidays. Sumo wrestling is just as popular as baseball. Traditional and simple pleasures—such as flower arranging, gardening, and tea drinking—have always been enjoyed by the Japanese.

If you took a traditional bath Japanese style, it would be quite different from taking one in America. You would be given a small wooden bucket and a washcloth. You soap your body outside the tub and rinse off with water from the bucket. Only when you are completely clean do you settle into a very hot tub for a long, relaxing soak. Afterwards, completely refreshed, you would put on a *yukata*, which is a cotton kimono.

Kimonos

The kimono is Japan's traditional clothing for women. An *obi*, or sash, is used to tie the loose-fitting garment. Since World War II, most Japanese have worn western-style clothing for daily wear. However, kimonos of darker colors are still worn by some older persons. Japanese wear simple kimonos for special celebrations and festivals, Japanese women of all ages wear the finest and most colorful of these garments.

Young Japanese women look forward to being fitted for their first fine kimono. A Japanese woman will also probably wear a special wedding kimono when she marries.

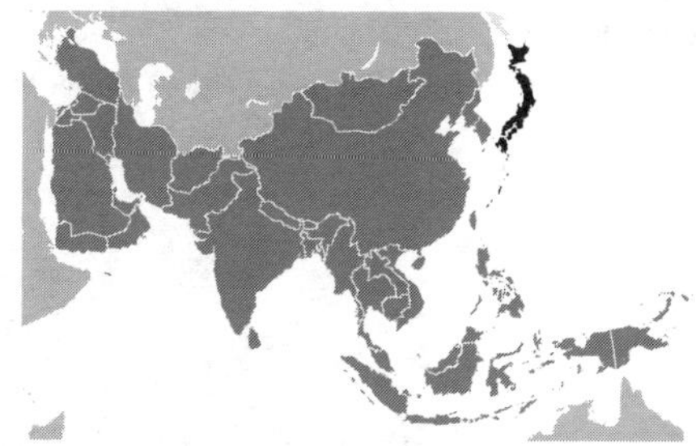

Chapter 1 – Japan

Words to Know

harmony:
in pleasant agreement

Japanese Values

One American characteristic that the Japanese have not adopted is casualness. They act in a very formal, polite way and place great value on honesty, kindness, and cooperation. The Japanese are respectful to others and try to live in **harmony** with people and nature. When they greet others, they show their respect by bowing. They tend to avoid speaking harshly to others or causing another person embarrassment.

People in Japan cooperate in gardening, flower arranging, sports, school, and even sightseeing groups. The Japanese put the interest of the group before the interest of the individual. This unselfish attitude towards working together helps keep peace among the people living in the crowded conditions that exist throughout the country.

Family Life

In the past, large extended families lived together in the same house. Sometimes uncles and aunts, as well as grandparents, were part of the same household. The husband was head of the entire family. Children were expected to obey their parents and those in authority. The parents chose marriage partners for their children.

Today, the family units of Japan are much smaller. Elderly parents may still live with the family. One reason for the smaller family is that apartments and houses in the cities are small. Young people are free to choose their own marriage partners, but most will not marry without their parents' approval.

Many Japanese women now hold jobs outside the family. About 40 percent of the workers are women, and this number is growing steadily. But men, not women, hold the most important jobs in Japan. This is unlike the United States, where some women hold important positions in large corporations.

In Japan it is difficult for a woman to have children as well as work outside the home. Businesses there expect employees to work many extra hours every week, so childcare is a problem. As a result, fewer Japanese women are choosing to have children.

Life in Rural Japan

About 25 percent of the people of Japan now live in rural areas. Back in 1960, about 30 percent lived in rural areas. In recent years, large numbers of people have moved to the cities, where there are more jobs. This has caused the cities to become very crowded. The government is trying to interest workers in remaining in rural areas.

Farmers use the latest farming methods and modern machinery. The use of fertilizers and other farm-related chemicals has greatly increased crop production in recent years. Farmers now have more time, and some hold additional jobs in nearby cities.

Many Japanese women, such as these factory assembly workers, now have jobs outside the home.

LESSON REVIEW

Directions: Number your paper from 1 to 5. Then answer the following questions.

1. Give two examples of the influence of Western countries on Japanese life.
2. What is a kimono? When is it worn?
3. Why has farm production increased in modern years?
4. Compare family life in the past to family life in modern Japan.
5. Why do you think Japanese values—such as politeness, honesty, and cooperation—are still highly valued by the Japanese?

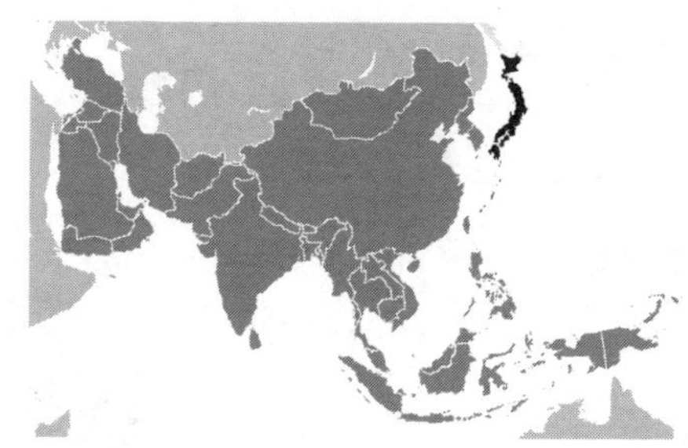

Words to Know

contrast:
to compare differences

LESSON 4: City Living

Japanese cities, like American ones, are large and very crowded. They have tall buildings, modern roads, and busy business districts. Buses, subways, and taxis are used to move people around the cities. Some people take the *Shinkasen*, known as bullet trains, to get to their jobs. This railroad system connects Japan's four main islands.

The Shinkasen, *or bullet trains, take people where they want to go.*

Contrasting housing styles can be seen throughout Japan. Tall apartment buildings and traditional Japanese houses of one or two stories with beautiful gardens can be found in the cities. Other people live in Western-style houses. These houses are also small and usually have one or two rooms decorated in the traditional Japanese style. Although there are some poor neighborhoods in the cities, there are few slums.

Problems in the Cities

Many people are moving to the cities because jobs are plentiful. The people work in banks, factories, hotels, offices, restaurants, and shops. Many people own their own businesses. There are also many government jobs and opportunities for professional people, such as doctors and lawyers.

The number of people moving to the cities is causing an overpopulation problem. For example, about 25 percent of the population of Japan lives in the greater Tokyo area! Two other major problems are lack of housing and pollution of the air and water. Crime is not a major problem in Japanese cities. In fact, it is claimed that among big cities in the world, Tokyo is the safest.

Shopping in Japan

When Japanese teenagers go shopping, many of the girls wear the same jeans and T-shirts commonly seen in the United States. As in America, the malls in Japan are lively and colorful, even to the point of having a carnival-like atmosphere. If you are homesick for some good old American fast food—don't despair! You will probably see some familiar restaurants to satisfy your cravings.

Unique aspects of Japanese malls include the games that visitors can play. These areas are similar to arcades in the United States. However, being an American, you may find that the games are somewhat unusual.

When you go to a mall in Japan, at first you might think that you are in the United States. The trend there, as well as here, is to meet friends at shopping malls. Shopping is definitely a social event!

Japan Is an Industrial Country

Together with the United States and Western Europe, Japan has one of the most powerful market economies in the world today. Japan's products include oil tankers, automobiles, and heavy machinery. Japanese electronic products are known worldwide. You may even own Japanese-made radios, tape recorders, calculators, computers, televisions, and VCRs. Japanese precision instruments—such as cameras, binoculars, and clocks—are famous for their high quality. Only the United States produces more manufactured goods than Japan.

Japan has the second-largest fishing industry in the world. Large amounts of tuna and salmon are caught, along with octopus, squid, crabs, and shrimp. In recent years, pollution of the waters along the coast has caused a decrease in the amount of fish caught. Another factor affecting deep-sea fishing is the enforcement by many nations of a limit on where fishing can be done.

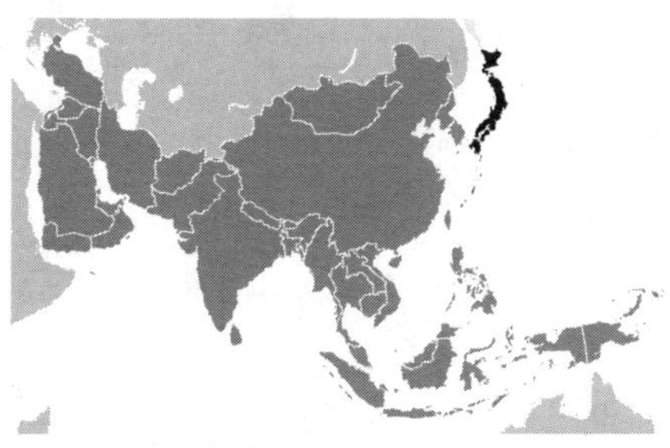

CHAPTER 1 – JAPAN

Words to Know

technical:
having to do with mechanical or industrial ability

Changes in Employment Security

In the past, Japanese workers in large companies could expect to be employed for life. But in the 1990s, companies started making less money, so they laid off workers. The workers could no longer count on having a job at the same company for the rest of their lives. Now jobs and salaries are based more on how well a worker does a job and less on how long a worker has been with a company.

Unemployment is low. Most Japanese workers feel loyal to their companies. Workers attend company meetings and learn company slogans and songs. When companies do well, they pay workers more money or give them better working conditions. This encourages workers to do the best job they can.

Reason for Japan's Success

Japan became a successful industrial country after World War II. Many countries, including the United States, shared their **technical** knowledge with Japan to help rebuild its industries. The Japanese have used this advantage and are now the most highly skilled workers in the world. As a result, the manufactured goods they produce are of high quality. Japan ships goods to markets around the world.

Today, the United States and Japan are trading partners. This means that American goods are sold in Japan and Japanese goods can be sold in America. However, there is an imbalance in this agreement. Japan sends more goods to the United States than the United States sends to Japan. Both the United States and Japan are trying to bring more balance to their trade agreements.

LESSON REVIEW

Directions: Number your paper from 1 to 5. Then answer the following questions.

1. What is the Shinkasen?
2. What are two problems in the cities of Japan?
3. Why was Japan successfully able to rebuild its industries after World War II?
4. Why has air and water pollution become a problem in Japan in recent years?
5. Why do you think Japanese workers feel loyalty to their companies? Explain your answer.

LESSON 5: Education in Japan

Education is important in Japan. Eight percent of the government budget is used for this purpose. Almost all adult Japanese can read and write. A degree from a college or university almost guarantees a person a good job in the government or in business. Japanese parents are very involved in their children's education. They spend much time staying in contact with teachers and seeing that their children take their studies seriously.

By law, young people must complete six years of elementary school and three years of junior high school. In the early years of school, students study such things as art, music, physical education, mathematics, and social studies. They must spend a lot of time studying the Japanese language because it is so difficult. A foreign language, often English, is also studied. Students must pass an entrance examination to be allowed to go on to a senior high school. About 96 percent of junior high students continue their schooling. After senior high, students may prepare themselves for a job by going on to a higher education. However, only about 46 percent of the students go on to colleges or universities because there are not enough places for all students.

As in the United States, public education is free during the elementary and junior high school years. The school week has been 5 1/2 days, but there are some changes taking place. There are now two free Saturdays a month, with a trend toward a five-day school week.

Since the government pays for children's education, it expects hard work and good behavior from the students. In recent years, there has been an increase in emotional and behavioral problems in students at all grade levels. Some blame the educational system for being too strict

There are not enough places for all students to attend college.

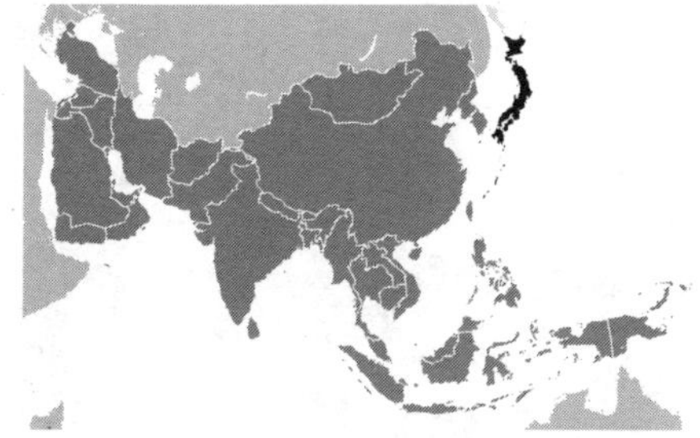

Words to Know

ritual:
a ceremony that is performed as part of a special occasion, often as a religious tradition

Christan:
the religion based on a belief in Jesus Christ and on the Old Testament and New Testament of the bible as sacred scripture

and putting too much pressure on students. In 1997, the Ministry of Education started a program to reform education. They want to decrease pressure on the students and improve their well-being.

Many demands are made on the teachers, too. They must encourage their students to give enough attention to their studies in order to succeed. They must also see that their students behave both inside and outside school. Even during vacation, teachers check on their students to see that they are attending to their assignments as they should. Can you imagine a teacher checking on your studies during the summer?

Religion in Japan

Many Japanese still follow Buddhist and Shinto traditions. These religious **rituals** can still be seen in special ceremonies or festivals, such as weddings, funerals, or holidays.

Shinto, which is practiced by most people, is the country's traditional religion. It is a joyful religion. The Japanese love of nature can be seen in their religion. They worship parts of nature like rivers, trees, and rocks. They also worship their ancestors.

A large number of Japanese practice Buddhism as well as Shinto. Buddhism came to Japan from China and Korea in the sixth century. Many of the people observe parts of both religions. Buddhists believe that material things are unimportant. They think that leading a wise and good life is most important. They also believe that a person, after living many lives of pain and unhappiness, may finally exist in a state of perfect peace and happiness.

The Tokugawas made **Christianity** illegal in the seventeenth century. Today, less than one percent of the Japanese are Christians. However, Christians are respected by the general population because they have been actively involved in education and social work and are considered by many to be people of the best moral character.

LESSON REVIEW

Directions: Number your paper from 1 to 4. Then answer the following questions.

1. What is the role of the parents in children's education?
2. What percent of Japanese students go on to college? Why?
3. What do Shintoists worship?
4. Why do you think Japanese students and parents are serious about education, even in elementary school?

LESSON 6: Having Fun in Japan

Do you read poetry to your friends? The Japanese do! Japan's most famous poet was Matsuo Basho. This samurai gave up the life of a warrior to write and teach poetry. His poems were about small events in nature or about animals.

The greatest work of Japanese fiction is the novel *The Tale of Genji* by Murasaki Shikibu. Written in A.D. 1000, it tells about the scandals and intrigues of life in the royal courts during that time. Interest in the arts extends beyond writing. Wooden block prints are also popular in Japan. Some pictures printed from these blocks are made with only one color, but some are made with many colors. Prints with many colors became popular in the late 1700s. The pictures were often of beautiful women, actors, or mothers and children. Landscape prints became popular in the early 1800s. A famous artist, Hokusai, produced his well-known set of prints called *Thirty-six Views of Mt. Fuji*. They showed the famous snow-capped Mount Fuji.

In addition, the Japanese paint on scrolls. Some of the paintings use very few brush strokes and leave much of the picture blank. The paintings are usually of simple parts of nature, such as bamboo or a bird. Some Japanese artists painted large scrolls. They often told stories or showed historical events, such as battles. These scrolls are often hung for display.

The Japanese appreciate plays as well as art. The oldest drama form the Japanese enjoy is the No Play. It has no more than five actors who use simple movements to tell a story. A chorus is often accompanied by drums and flutes. The stage is small and bare. The actors wear colorful costumes and use wooden masks that show different feelings.

During the late 1600s, two other important forms of drama were developed—the puppet theater and the Kabuki play. Puppet plays use large, life-like puppets to act out the story as it is told by a narrator. Kabuki plays are dramatic and tell about events in history or everyday life. Kabuki Theater uses colorful scenery, as well as music, dancing, costumes, and heavy makeup. The acting style is lively and exaggerated. In the older Kabuki plays, the only actors in the play were men. They played all the parts: men, women, and even animals. In modern Kabuki plays, women perform some roles.

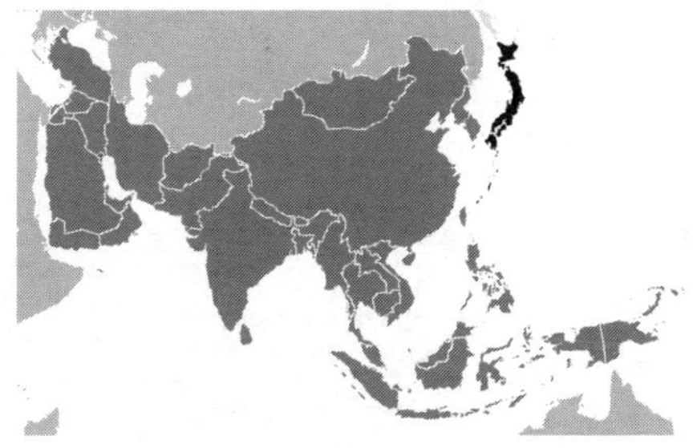

Haiku

One of the best-liked forms of poetry in Japan is haiku. A haiku is a short poem that does not rhyme. It has three lines with only seventeen syllables. The first line has five syllables; the second, seven; and the last, five. Sometimes, when haikus are translated into English, the number of syllables is different from the original.

This haiku poem is by Basho, Japan's favorite poet:

> The summer grasses —
> Of brave soldiers' dreams
> The aftermath.

Recreation

Young Japanese people like the same types of recreational activities as people in America. Western music of all kinds is very popular. Watching television is another enjoyable pastime. Favorite shows include news, drama, comedy, and quiz shows. A popular educational network in Japan allows the home audience to take part in programs. Home computers can be linked up to a computer in the television studio. By pushing a button, a viewer can get medical advice, community news, recipes, and shopping advice. Classes are taught on TV, and the viewers can be tested by using this same computer link-up.

The Japanese are interested in current events and news, and there are several national newspapers. Japanese newspapers have fewer pages than American papers because little advertising is used. News stories cover events that are happening in all parts of the world.

Sightseeing, mountain climbing, and hiking are all popular pastimes with the Japanese. They also enjoy visiting amusement parks. In 1985 Disneyland was built near Tokyo. This popular attraction is just like Disneyland in California.

Many people enjoy sightseeing in Japan.

Sports

Almost all sports enjoyed by people in Western nations are also played in Japan. The most popular is baseball. Two professional leagues include a total of 12 teams. Baseball is also played in schools and colleges.

Other sports enjoyed by many are soccer, volleyball, swimming, and skiing. Bowling is becoming popular. Golf is played mainly by the wealthy. Sumo wrestling is the most popular native sport. The wrestlers are extremely heavy, some weighing 300 pounds. They tie their hair in the traditional topknot.

Sumo wrestling is popular in Japan.

LESSON REVIEW

Directions: Number your paper from 1 to 5. Then answer the following questions.

1. Describe Haiku poetry.
2. Block prints are popular. What are some favorite subjects of these prints?
3. Describe the two drama forms that developed after 1600.
4. Compare Japanese newspapers to American newspapers.
5. Why do you think baseball, rather than football or another sport, is so popular in Japan?

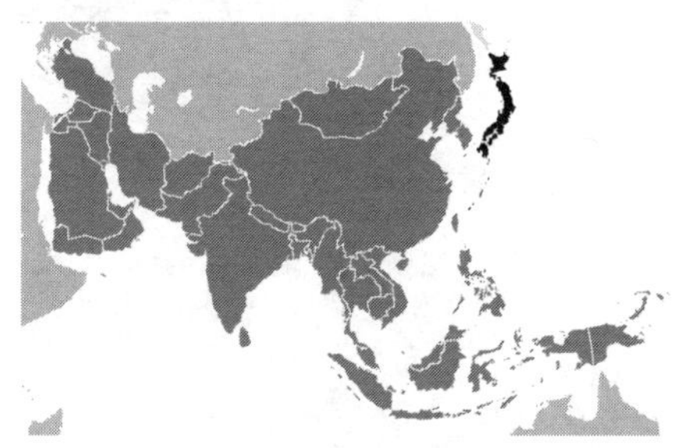

Words to Know

futon:
a quilt-like mattress placed on the floor and used as a bed

hibachi:
a grill that holds and burns charcoal for cooking or heating

Spotlight Story

Visiting the Ioki Family

I was nervous and excited at the Tokyo airport. Two members of my host family, Mr. Ioki and his daughter, Naoki, were waiting for me. We took the bullet train to a station close to their home.

At their house, Mrs. Ioki welcomed me to Japan. We laughed as I attempted to talk to her in broken Japanese. Before entering their home, I removed my shoes and put on slippers. This custom helps to keep the house clean. Unfortunately, my large American feet didn't fit into the small Japanese slippers very well.

We went into the *cha-no-ma*, literally, "tea room," and were served a cold drink and watermelon—a very costly treat in Japan. The family's friendly gestures made me feel like an old friend.

In the Ioki home the walls separating the rooms are made of lightweight wood and paper. Mr. Ioki explained that before central heating was popular, the only heat came from the *kotatsu*, which was a pit in the floor of one room. It contained a charcoal-burning **hibachi**. A low table was placed over the kotatsu and a quilt was put over the table. The family sat around the area, with their feet under the quilt to keep warm.

Mrs. Ioki announced that dinner was ready. The food was very colorful and was arranged beautifully on the plate. I was told that "we Japanese eat food not only with our mouths, but with our eyes." Tea, a favorite drink, was served with our meal.

We ate rice and two Japanese delicacies, sashimi and sushi. Both of these dishes are made with raw fish! We dipped the fish slices into a small dish of soy sauce, a salty sauce made from soybeans. It was challenging to eat my meal with chopsticks!

Later that night I slept on a Japanese **futon** on the floor. These quilt-like mattresses are folded up and put out of sight in the daytime.

SPOTLIGHT REVIEW

Answer the following questions.

1. Before central heating in houses, how did the Japanese keep warm?
2. Describe the inside of the traditional Japanese house.
3. Name three favorite foods of the Japanese.
4. Describe how the Japanese serve and eat their meals.
5. What is the favorite drink served with meals?

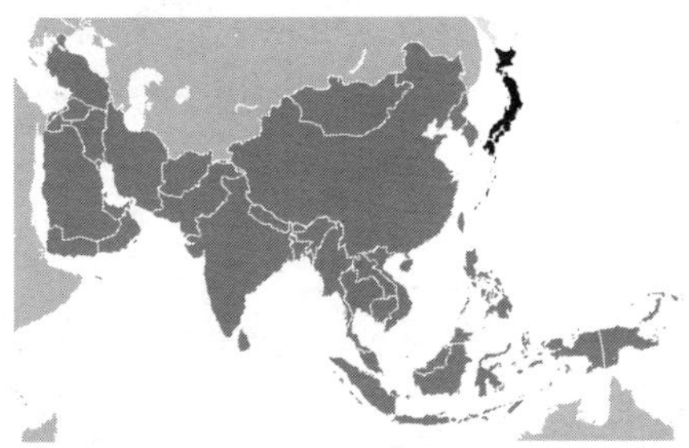

Chapter 1 Review

Japan is a mountainous country made up of thousands of islands. In Japan's early years, powerful families or military leaders ruled. The Meiji period marked the beginning of modern Japan. Under the leadership of Emperor Mutsuhito, many positive changes and advancements were made.

Japan has seen its share of war. During World War II, Japan was an ally of Germany. At the end of World War II, Japan was totally destroyed and had to rebuild its industries and government. With the help of the United States and others, it succeeded. Today, Japan is a modern, industrial country. Even though Western influence is strong, the Japanese have maintained many customs of their own culture. Japanese cities are very crowded; about 25 percent of the people in Japan live in or near Tokyo. Education is important to all Japanese.

This is a classic Japanese landscape.

Critical Thinking Skills

Directions: Give some thought to the questions below. Be sure to answer in complete sentences.

1. If you were visiting Japan, what are some traditional Japanese activities that you might experience?
2. What are two problems found in many United States cities that are not found in Japanese cities?
3. If a Japanese student attended school in the United States, what differences would he/she notice between the two educational systems?
4. Compare television in Japan to television in the United States.

For Discussion

1. Why did the Allies feel that it was necessary to take control of Japan after World War II?
2. Japanese companies share any progress made with their employees. How do you think this is done?
3. Why do you think men hold most executive jobs in large corporations in Japan, although 40 percent of the women are part of the work force?
4. The influence of Western culture is very evident in Japan. Why do you think this is so?
5. Many important forms of drama developed in Japan over the years. If you visited Japan, describe the drama form that you would like to see performed.

Write It!

Directions: You are planning a dinner for your Japanese friend. You want her to feel at home. You will be serving some Japanese dishes. Plan a menu for the dinner. Discuss how you will set the table. Use a Japanese cookbook to help you.

For You to Do

Directions: Plan a trip to Tokyo, Japan. Use the library and local travel agents to find out pertinent information. Using a map, trace the route and possible stops and/or side trips.

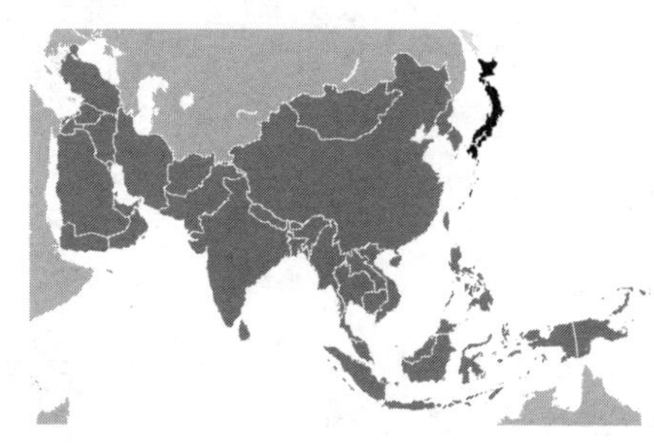

KOREA

CHAPTER 2

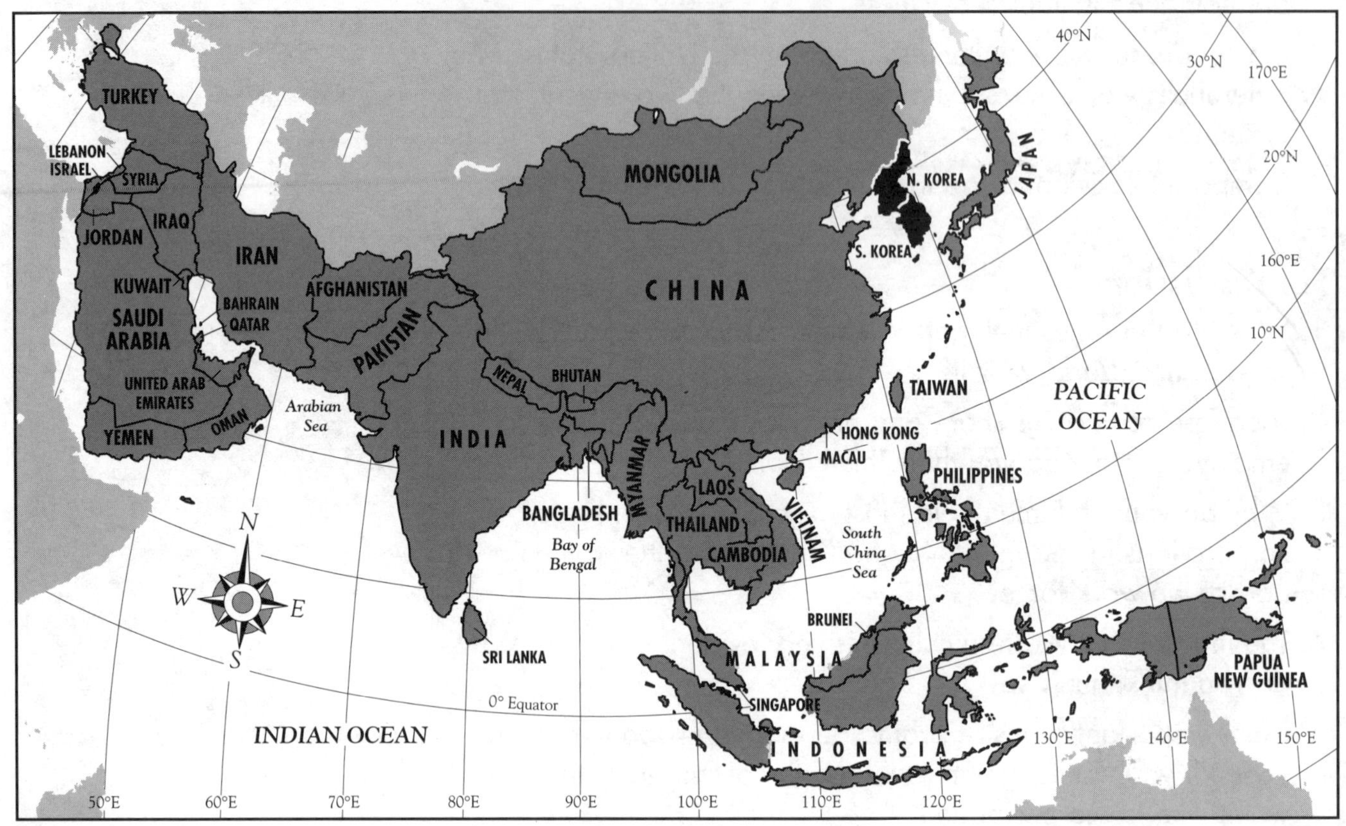

Fast Facts

- Korea is really two countries: South Korea and North Korea.
- Koreans invented the world's first metal printing press.
- Mask dances are the most common kind of folk dance in Korea.
- The capital of South Korea is Seoul; the capital of North Korea is Pyongyang.

CHAPTER 2 – KOREA

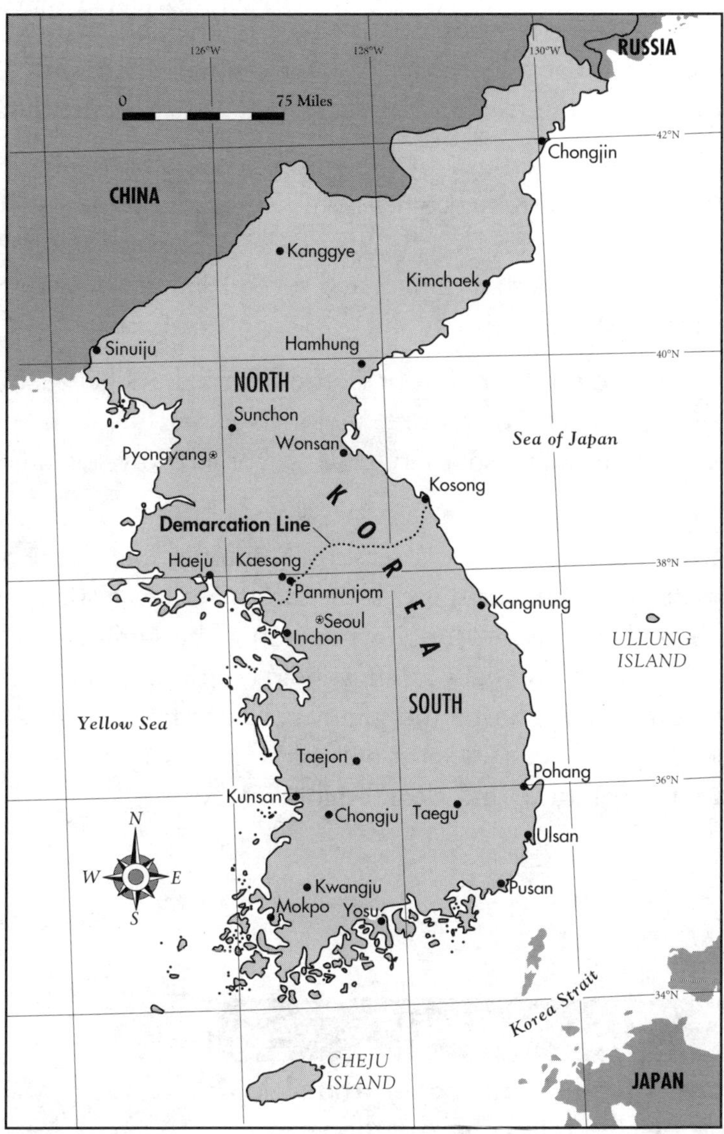

MAP SKILLS

The Two Koreas (Using Parts of a Map)

Directions: Study the map above to answer these questions.

1. What is the dividing line between North and South Korea called?
2. What body of water separates South Korea from Japan?
3. What country is northwest of Korea?
4. What country is northeast of Korea?

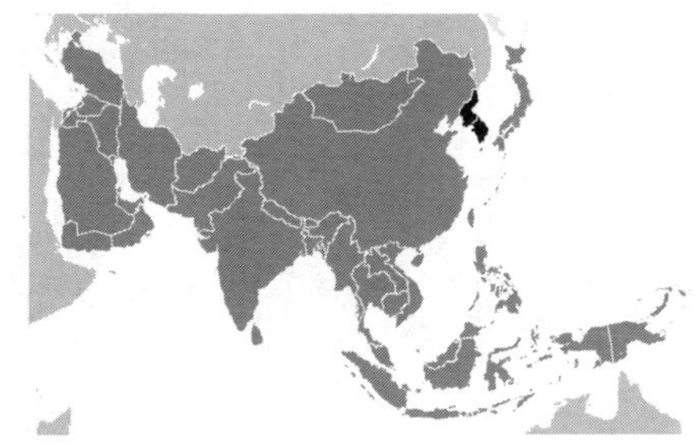

Chapter 2 – Korea

Words to Know

Communist:
a person who supports communism, in which most property is owned by the state, or government

dynasty:
rulers belonging to the same family

moderate:
describing a person who avoids extremes

LESSON 1: The Peninsula of Korea

Korea is really two countries. South Korea is a republic. North Korea is under **Communist** rule. In this chapter you will learn ways in which these two countries are the same, and ways they are different.

Korea is a peninsula with many mountains located between China and Japan. The word *Korea* comes from *Koryo*, which means "high and beautiful." Korea bridges the ocean waters between China and Japan. Two large mountain ranges and several smaller ones run the length of the peninsula.

Most people live on the plains or in the river valleys between these mountain ranges. There are three major rivers in the north and three in the south. The southern coast is bordered by several thousand islands.

The Korean Peninsula has four seasons. Winter is cold in the whole country, although the north is colder than the south. Spring rains bring the moisture needed for growing crops. The summers are hot and wet. The rains and melting snow help crops, but they can also cause flooding. Also, during the summer the southern coast is often threatened by typhoons. A short but colorful fall season has **moderate** temperatures and clear, bright weather.

LESSON REVIEW

Directions: Number your paper from 1 to 4. Then answer the following questions.

1. What are the two parts of Korea?
2. What does the word Korea mean?
3. What two countries is Korea between?
4. In what area do most people in Korea live?

CHAPTER 2 – KOREA

This Korean village is surrounded by rice fields.

Koreans at Home

Since ancient times, Koreans have shown respect for their elders and ancestors. Older people in households get special attention, especially on their 60th birthday. A child's first birthday is also reason to celebrate.

Koreans value comfort in their homes. Many Korean homes and apartments have a heating system that heats the floor. The rising heat keeps the whole room warm. Koreans sit on the floor and eat at low tables, so dining rooms are not needed. Some still sleep on the floor, so bedrooms are not necessary. Eating and sleeping equipment is put away for the day. This way, a family can live together in a small space.

Family life in South Korea has changed very little in recent years. In North Korea, however, most women now work outside their homes. This means that they must leave their children in government nurseries while they are at work. If a South Korean woman had a job outside her home, some family member would probably take care of the children.

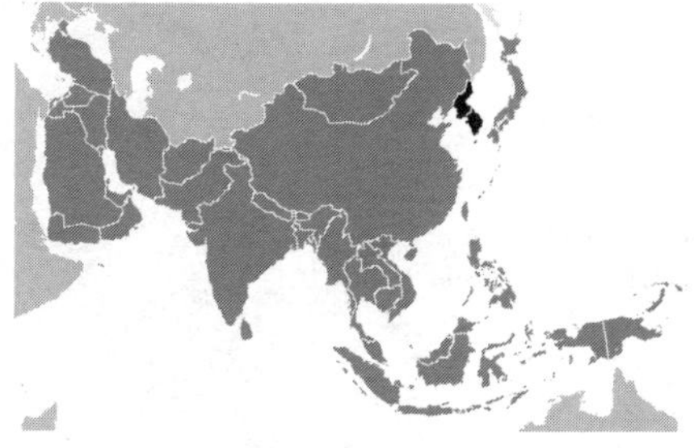

Words to Know

dialect:
a certain form of a spoken language

shaman:
a person believed to have close contact with the spirit world; medicine man

LESSON 2: The History of Korea

Korea is an ancient land. During the first century A.D., Korea was known as Choson. The people of the Korean peninsula were organized into three large kingdoms: the Koguryo, the Paekche, and the Silla. By the seventh century A.D., one government, the Silla, and one major religion, Buddhism, had been established.

Through the centuries, Korea's history was marked by violence. The armies of Japan and China invaded Korea many times. From 1910 to 1945, Japan ruled Korea. After Japan's defeat at the end of World War II, Russia took control of the northern part of the country. There they set up a Communist government.

The southern part of Korea was independent. The Communists in the north, with the help of China, tried to take over the south. The United States and other countries of the United Nations came to the aid of South Korea. From 1950 to 1953, there was a war between the two sides. At the end of the war, Korea was still a divided country.

Although both sides signed a truce, they never signed a peace treaty. They agreed to create a border that would divide the north part of Korea from the southern part. They called this border the Demarcation Line. The land on either side of the line is the Demilitarized Zone (DMZ). It would be free from the threat of military attack. This zone is two and a half miles wide. It stretches across the peninsula near the 38th parallel. In the years since this zone was created, the two sides have had many talks. They have not reached any agreement to end this division.

LESSON REVIEW

Directions: Number your paper from 1 to 4. For each question, write *T* for true or *F* for false.

1. During the first century A.D., the Korean people were organized into six large kingdoms.
2. The border between North and South Korea is called the Demarcation Line.
3. The leaders of the countries signed a peace treaty after the Korean War.
4. The history of Korea has been very peaceful.

LESSON 3: The People of Korea

The Koreans, like the Japanese, are of the Asian race, but of a different ethnic group. They have a culture all their own. They have copied ideas and customs from neighboring countries, such as China and Japan. Koreans speak one language, which has six **dialects**. Most Koreans can understand all of the dialects. Their alphabet is believed to be one of the most scientific systems of writing ever developed. Korea is also credited with having the world's first metal printing press. It was invented 50 years before Johannes Gutenberg's press in Germany.

When the Choson Dynasty (1392-1910) was established, Seoul became Korea's capital. This ancient city is still the capital of South Korea. It is home to 24 percent of the country's population of 47 million. It is the largest city in the world. North Korea has a population of 21 million. Its capital, Pyongyang, is home to 2,600,000 of those people.

Koreans love nature, family, and their social order. All of these show the influence of the philosophy of Confucius. They are proud of their beautiful country with its mountains and rivers. Many Koreans no longer believe in the spirit world. But the influence of ancient **shamans**, people thought capable of communicating with the spirits in nature, still exists. Koreans are very aware of how they treat all of nature, both plant and animal.

The social order of the past was based on a person's job, not on how much money they had. Today, a new social order has developed in Korea. Because many people have gotten an education, they are able to find jobs that bring them economic security. These jobs are mostly in the city. The lower classes in rural areas still earn a living by farming.

This family enjoys grocery shopping together.

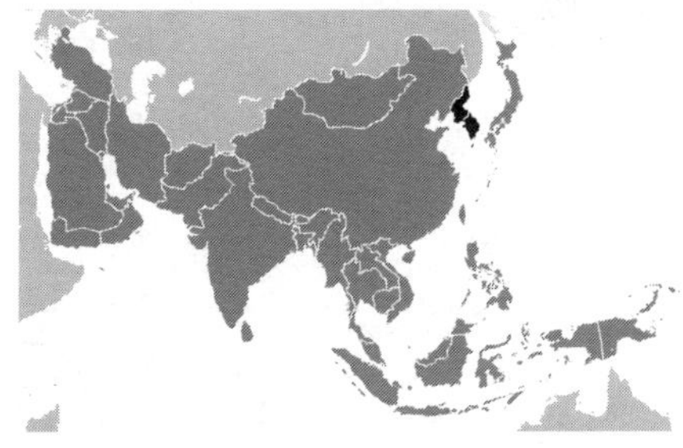

Words to Know

acupuncture:
an ancient Chinese practice of inserting needles into certain parts of the body to treat disease or relieve pain

In North Korea, the government provides medical care to the people. Unfortunately, there are not enough doctors or hospitals for them. In South Korea, at least half the people have health insurance, but they, too, have a shortage of doctors and hospitals. Koreans use traditional ways of healing, such as herbs and **acupuncture**. But they practice Western medicine, too.

Koreans in the cities wear mostly western-style clothing. There are a few people in rural areas who still wear traditional Korean attire. For men, this is full pants, a short jacket or vest, a coat, and sometimes a tall hat. For women, traditional dress is a long, full skirt and a short jacket or blouse with a sash. Many citizens in both North and South Korea wear traditional costumes for special celebrations.

LESSON REVIEW

Directions: Number your paper from 1 to 4. Then answer the following questions.

1. What was the social order of the past based on?
2. Do any Koreans still wear traditional Korean clothing? When do they wear it?
3. What is the shortage in both North Korea and South Korea that affects the health care the citizens receive?
4. Where are most of the better-paying jobs located?

The world's oldest astronomical observatory is in Silla, Korea.

Kim Dae-Jung, left, and Kim Jong Il, right, at their historic meeting.

An Important Meeting

A very important meeting took place in June 2000, nearly 50 years after the Korean War started.

The president of North Korea, Kim Jong II, said that he wanted to meet with the president of South Korea, Kim Dae-Jung. North Korea was suffering from severe food shortages and needed help.

The leaders of North Korea and South Korea met for the first time in North Korea's capital, Pyongyang. They agreed that the two countries should settle their differences and make their relationship more friendly. They decided to work together for the economic good of both countries.

Also, many families had been separated for 50 years. Some family members lived in North Korea, and some lived in South Korea. They were not allowed to see each other for all that time. After the meeting of the two presidents, many families were allowed to visit with one another.

The two countries hope that their relationship will continue to improve.

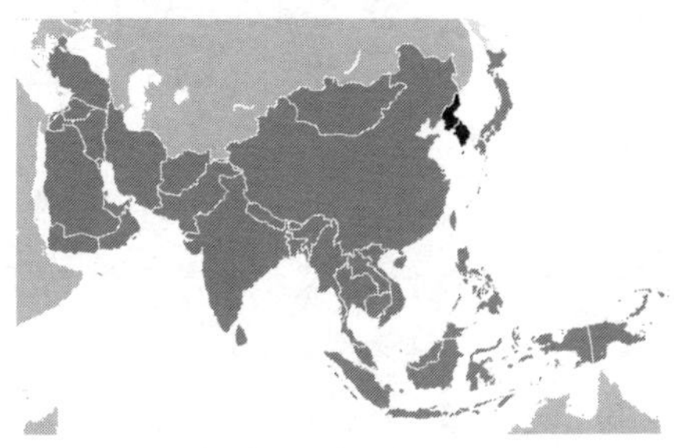

Words to Know

prosper:
to be successful

famine:
a food shortage that causes starvation

LESSON 4: Government and the Economy

After the Korean War, the United Nations decided that all of Korea should have free elections. South Korea became a democratic republic with two major political parties. After many years of military rule, the constitution was changed to establish three branches of government. These branches are the executive, the legislative, and the judicial. People are elected to serve in the legislative branch. The national government appoints provincial officials. Freedom in South Korea makes protest possible, and students often protest against government officials.

North Korea also has a constitution that establishes three branches. These branches are the Supreme People's Assembly, the Central People's Committee, and the State Administration Council. The Supreme People's Assembly has almost unlimited power. In Communist North Korea, the only important political party is the Korean Worker Party.

Since the mid-1950s, South Korea's economy has grown a great deal (except during the 1998 financial crisis). It has become one of the world's biggest exporting and trading nations. The United States is its largest overseas customer. As the country **prospered**, it needed more roads and buildings. Many people had jobs building these roads and buildings, and all these jobs helped the economy grow.

South Korea is a world leader as a fishing nation. Farming isn't as important as it once was, but many small farms still grow rice. Many people, especially young people, have moved from farms to the cities, because there are more jobs in the cities.

We don't know very much about the economy in North Korea. The Communist government does not give out much information about industry. It does little trading with the Western world, and the products it manufactures are a lower quality than those from South Korea. North Korea manufactures machinery, tractors, and weapons to use and to send to China.

North Korea has many mineral deposits. Among the minerals they export are ore, zinc, and lead. Coal mining is important, because much of the country's electricity is produced by factories powered by coal. Mountain forests of fir and spruce trees supply timber for the country.

North Korea has several thousand farms that are owned by the government. A little more than 40 percent of the people who work are in agriculture. The two main crops are corn and rice. The country's farms cannot produce enough food for all the people in North Korea, so some food must come from other countries. There was a terrible **famine** in the mid-1990s, so other nations had to help provide food. Just as in South Korea, fishing is important to North Korea's economy.

Some people have encouraged North and South Korea to work together to help the economies of both countries. However, North Korea has a long way to go to catch up with South Korea in production and international trade.

LESSON REVIEW

Directions: Number your paper from 1 to 5. Then answer the following questions.

1. What are the three branches of government in South Korea?
2. What are the three branches of government in North Korea?
3. Why do many young South Koreans move from farms to cities?
4. What are the two main crops in North Korea?
5. What happened in the mid-1990s that had a terrible affect on the people of North Korea?

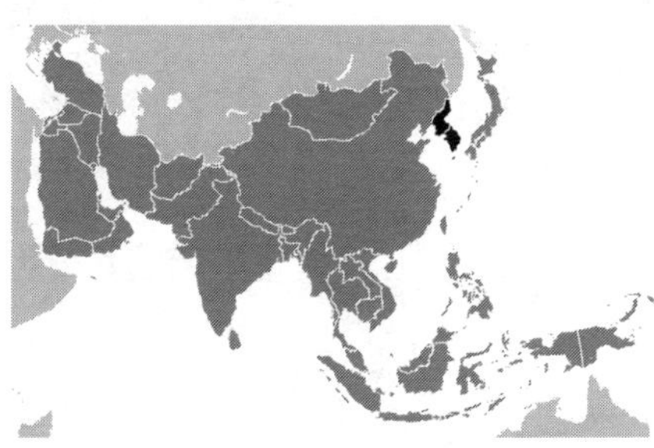

Words to Know

missionary:
a person sent out by their church, to convert people to their religious beliefs

LESSON 5: Religion

The teachings of the philosopher Confucius have been very important to the Koreans. Confucius taught that it was important to respect people in authority. Generally, Korean citizens respect their rulers, wives obey husbands, and the young are influenced by their elders.

The constitutions of both North and South Korea guarantee freedom of religion. Until recently, however, the North Korean government did not want people to practice religion. South Koreans are free to practice whatever religion they wish. Buddhism is one of the most popular religions. It is similar to the ancient religion of Korea, Shamanism, which honors the spirits of nature. Christianity was brought to Korea in the sixteenth century by **missionaries** and is practiced today by large numbers of South Koreans.

The teachings of Confucius have been very important to the Koreans.

LESSON REVIEW

Directions: Number your paper from 1 to 4. Then answer these questions.

1. The teachings of what philosopher have been very important to the Koreans?
2. What things did this philosopher teach?
3. What is one of the most popular religions in South Korea?
4. What religious belief honors the spirits of nature?

LESSON 6: Education and Sports

Kindergarten is not required in South Korea, but children may attend when they reach the age of five. Beginning at age seven, all children must attend elementary school. The government provides free schooling for students through grade six.

Children attend school year round, except for the hottest weeks of summer and the coldest weeks of winter. Until college, boys and girls attend classes separately. Physical education is taught along with academic studies. Students spend many hours in school and much time with homework.

All students may go to middle school, where they can take classes that prepare them for work in industry. Most students attend high school. Students must work very hard to pass exams to enter South Korea's colleges or universities. (In South Korea, students don't usually start dating until they are college age.)

Education begins early in North Korea. Government nurseries are provided for babies starting at three months until they are three or four years old. All school programs are planned by the government, and students must attend school for at least 11 years. They must also work for the government during the summer.

This modern sports complex was built for the 1988 Summer Olympics in Seoul, South Korea.

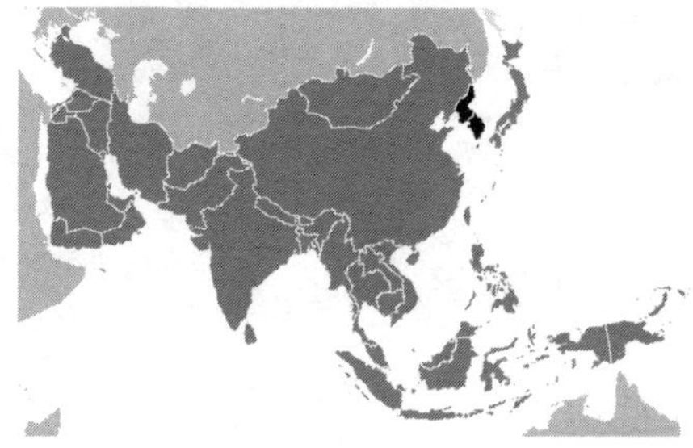

Students must also play a sport while in school, and they must learn a skill such as sewing or pottery-making. After ten years, students may attend vocational or technical school if they pass entrance exams. Good students can go on to college. The government offers classes for adults, and certain classes are required for factory workers as well.

Koreans have always enjoyed watching or participating in sports. Families spend time together outdoors hiking, swimming, or picnicking. In both North and South Korea, they participate in many of the same sports familiar to Americans. They play table tennis, soccer, volleyball, baseball, and archery. South Korea has professional baseball and soccer teams. Some people enjoy golf, boxing, or tennis. The sports of skiing, skating, and sledding are popular where the weather is cold. Children play on seesaws, spin tops, and fly kites. Adults play a board game very much like chess.

LESSON REVIEW

Directions: Number your paper from 1 to 4. Then answer the following questions.

1. At what age must all children begin elementary school in South Korea?
2. When do young people in South Korea start dating?
3. Who plans all the school programs in North Korea?
4. What are some of the sports that Koreans enjoy?

LESSON 7: Holidays, Festivals, and the Arts

Holidays and festivals are important to the Korean people. On the first two days of January in North Korea, and the first two weeks of February in South Korea, people celebrate the New Year. A special part of the holiday is the gathering of family and friends to pay respect to their ancestors. Concerts, games, and parades mark the Cherry Blossom Festival in April. In late April or May, Buddha's birthday is celebrated. People bring flowers and lanterns to the temples where they go to pray. On Children's Day, parents honor their children with gifts. The children wear costumes and play games.

Similar to our Thanksgiving, *Ch'usok* takes place in early fall. This is a time for family feasting and visiting the graves of ancestors. South Korean Christians celebrate Christmas.

Most other holidays in North Korea mark some political event. Some of these are the late President Kim Il Sung's birthday, Army Day, the founding of North Korea, and Party Foundation Day. These occasions are celebrated with sports events, political rallies, and banquets.

Fine arts are encouraged by the governments of both North and South Korea. In North Korea, all art must show good things about communism. It is just the opposite in South Korea, where art cannot encourage communism.

The arts are encouraged by both governments.

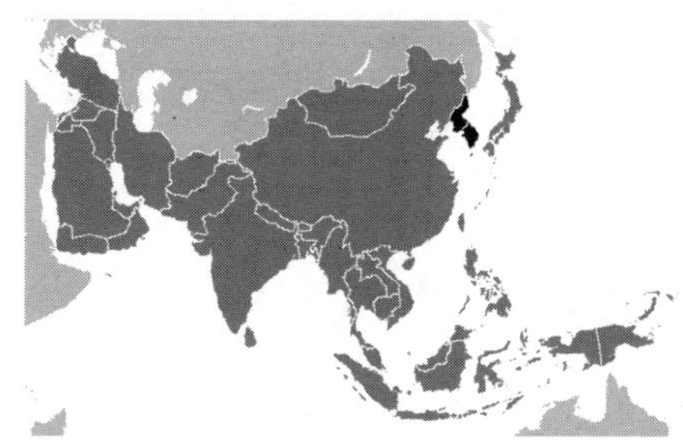

Through the centuries, Korean art has been influenced by Shamanism, Buddhism, and Confucianism. Painting, pottery, writing, music, and dance all show the effects of these religions. Artists are highly respected.

Classical Korean literature stresses history and nature. Sculpture, both ancient and modern, is an important Korean art form. Probably the best known Korean art form is pottery, especially celadon. Museums all over the world exhibit this pottery.

In Korea, there are two types of traditional music: *chongak* (music that was written for the noble people) and *sogak* (music written for common people). Folk music shows the influence of Buddhism and Shamanism. Korean dance includes folk dances, court dances, and mask dances. Mask dances are the most common kind of folk dances. The dancers wear masks that show greed, stupidity, and dishonesty of government or religious leaders.

LESSON REVIEW

Directions: Number your paper from 1 to 5. Then answer the following questions.

1. How do Koreans celebrate the Cherry Blossom Festival?
2. What festival is similar to Thanksgiving in the United States?
3. What do most holidays in North Korea celebrate?
4. What is one of the differences in art between North and South Korea?
5. What does classical Korean literature stress?

Spotlight Story

An Economic Crisis in Asia

The economic crisis started in 1997, when the economy of Thailand failed. This crisis soon spread to other Asian countries. Many Asian banks and businesses lost all their money.

Two main conditions led up to the crisis. First, many Asian businesses had borrowed money from banks. Then factories began producing more than they could sell. Prices went down. The businesses could not repay what they had borrowed. As a result, foreign investors got worried. They pulled their money out of Asia and invested it in other countries.

This economic crisis had a serious effect on North Korea, partly because the country was so closed off from the rest of the world. This crisis made the North Korean leaders realize that they should cooperate with other countries in order to help their own economy. North Korea joined the United Nations at that time to be in closer contact with the rest of the world.

In 1998 South Korea saw its economy begin to fail, along with the economies of other Asian countries. There had been too much business expansion and too little profit. Again, investors withdrew their money. South Korea, along with other Asian countries, received loans from the International Monetary Fund and other agencies. In order to get the money, these countries had to agree to use wiser business practices. Since that time, South Korea's economy has recovered and grown.

SPOTLIGHT REVIEW

Answer the following questions.

1. Where was the first sign of an economic crisis?
2. What conditions lead up to the 1997 crisis?
3. What action did North Korean leaders take as a result of the crisis?
4. What happened to cause the economy of South Korea to fail?
5. What did the Asian countries have to promise in order to get loans?

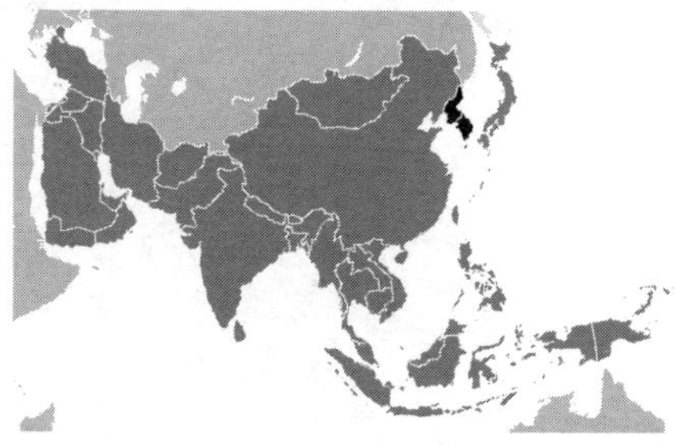

Chapter 2 Review

Korea is made up of South Korea, a republic, and North Korea, which is under Communist rule. The teachings of Confucius have been very important to the people of Korea.

The history of Korea has been marked by violence. From 1950 to 1953, there was a war between the two countries. Since then, North Korea has been isolated from the rest of the world.

South Korea's economy has grown in the last few decades, in spite of problems during the Asian financial crisis of the late 1990s. We don't know much about the economy in North Korea. The financial crisis caused extreme hardship for North Korea. A shortage of doctors is a problem for both of the countries.

In 2000, the leaders of the two countries met. They allowed families who have been split between the two countries to cross the border to visit. The future now looks more promising for cooperation between the two countries.

This Korean folk music is being performed the traditional way.

Chapter 2 – Korea

Critical Thinking Skills

Directions: Give some thought to the questions below. Be sure to answer in complete sentences.

1. Koreans show respect for their elders and ancestors. How is the United States or Canada similar in this way? How are they different?
2. Koreans are very much aware of how they treat nature. Do you find this attitude to be common where you live?
3. Do you think it's a good thing to have all school programs planned by the government?

For Discussion

1. What things could change in North Korea if the two countries agree to live peacefully and cooperate with each other?
2. Both North Korea and South Korea have governments with three different branches. Compare and contrast the two government systems.
3. Which of the sports listed in the chapter are familiar to you? Which ones would you like to try?

Write It!

Directions: If you could invent any kind of festival or celebration, what would it be? Describe when it would be celebrated and what you would do to observe the occasion. What foods would you eat? What costumes would you wear?

For You to Do

Directions: Korea is credited with inventing the world's first metal printing press. Using your library or Web resources, research printing presses. Find out how they are different from the way newspapers and magazines are produced today. Write a paragraph about these differences.

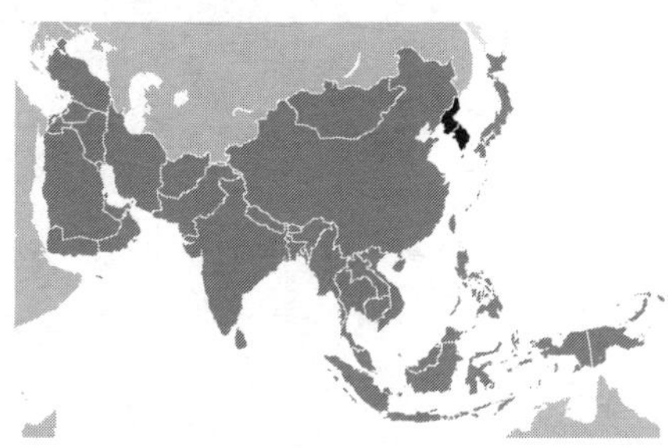

China

Chapter 3

Fast Facts

- One out of every five people in the world lives in China.
- The ancient Chinese invented paper, gunpowder, and the compass.
- The Great Wall of China can be seen from space.
- China was the home of the famous philosopher, Confucius.

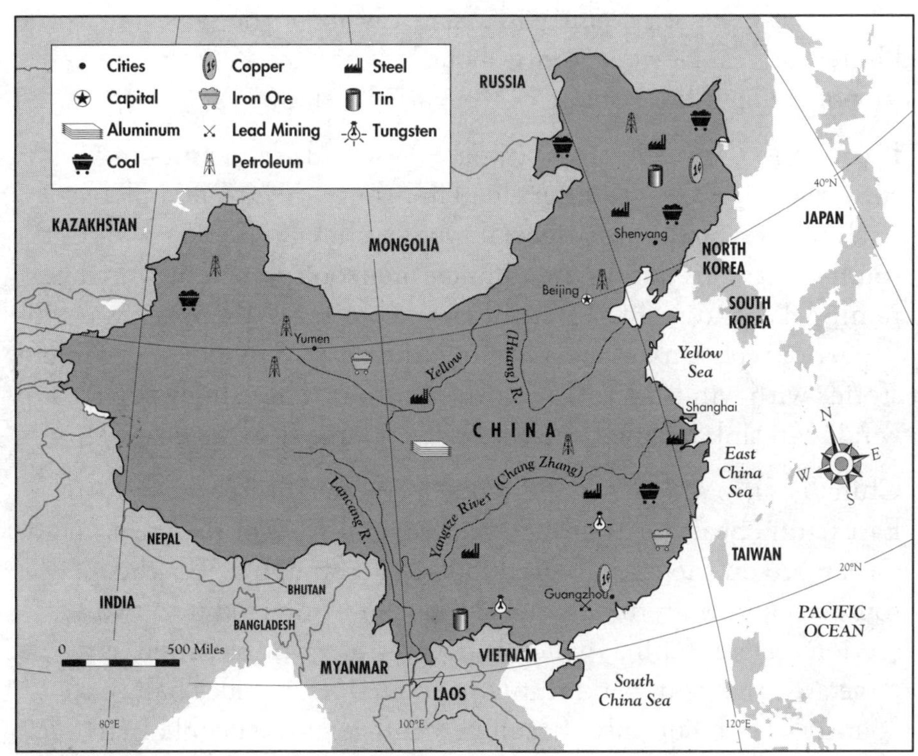

MAP SKILLS

Resources and Industrial Areas of China

Directions: Study the map above to answer these questions.

1. Name the products and resources listed in the northeastern area of China.
2. Name three rivers in China.
3. What industries and resources are located in the south near Guangzhou?
4. What two resources are found in the extreme northwestern part of China?
5. What busy industrial city is located at the mouth of the Chang Zhang?
6. Name two resources found near the city of Yumen.
7. Name the resources found near the cities of Beijing and Shenyang.

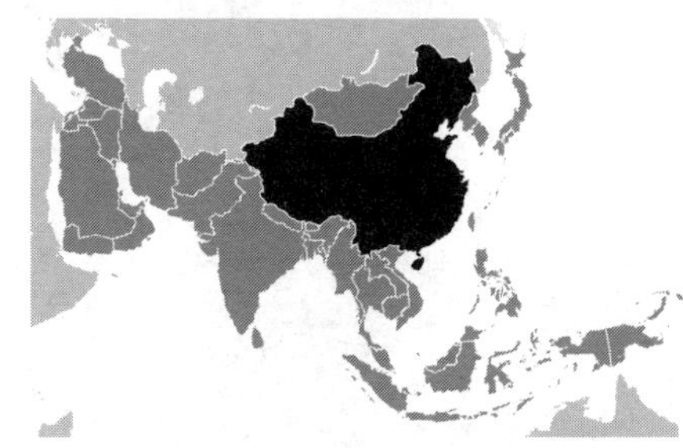

CHAPTER 3 – CHINA

> **Words to Know**
>
> **monsoon:**
> an Asiatic wind that blows from the southwest bringing rains from June to October
>
> **natural resources:**
> a form of wealth produced by nature, such as water power, coal, and oil
>
> **typhoon:**
> a violent storm with winds up 150 miles per hour

LESSON 1: A Look at the Vast Country of China

China is the largest country in Asia. It is about the same size as the United States. However, only about half of China's land can support human life because of the varied terrain.

If you were to travel across China, you would see mountains with snowcapped peaks, green fertile plains, huge deserts, and plateaus. Each of these areas has a special type of climate. If you travel to the southern regions during the summer **monsoon** season, it would be raining day and night. After these summer rains, there is always the danger of typhoons, especially along the coast. Typhoons are violent storms with winds up to 150 miles per hour. These high-powered winds can sink fishing boats and flatten large fields of crops.

China is surrounded by mountains or water. The Yellow Sea, the East China Sea, the South China Sea, and parts of the great Pacific Ocean are on the east. Rugged mountains stretch across the southern and western borders. China can be divided into two sections. Outer China, which is the western part of China, is a large area that is dry and thinly populated. It includes half of the country's land, but only a small percentage of the people live here. Inner China, the eastern region, is the most important part of China because of its farms and industries. Ninety percent of the Chinese people live in inner China.

If you visited this populated region of China, you might travel along the Chang Zhang or Yangtze River. It is one of the world's longest rivers and China's most important river. It is deep and wide enough for ocean-going vessels to travel over 600 miles up river to many industrial regions. Some smaller vessels can even travel 1,000 miles farther up river. Along this river can be seen many industrial and farming areas that help support China's millions of people.

The northern region of inner China is dusty and dry. In this area are hills and a large plateau called the Loess Plateau. Both are covered with a fine, yellow dust called loess, which is blown in from the desert. East of this plateau is a lowland plain formed by the Huang He or Yellow River. The plain is yellow in color because of the silt washed into it from the Loess Plateau.

The capital city of Beijing (Peking) is located in the fertile plain of the Huang He. Along the northern edge of the Huang He plain are hills and mountains. The famous Great Wall of China, built in ancient times to protect China from invaders, stretches across these hills.

These jagged peaks are a natural land feature in China.

The Manchurian Plain is northeast of the Great Wall and has some of the richest soil in China. Coal and other valuable minerals are **natural resources** found in this area. The Manchurian Plain is surrounded by mountains that have the best forests in China. Lumber from these forests is a major product of this region.

If you are among the few visitors who go to outer China, you would travel west of the mountains that border the Manchurian Plain. In this region is the high, rolling Mongolian Plateau that extends for about 1,000 miles. Short grass grows on this plateau to support flocks of sheep, goats, cattle, horses, and camels. Wandering shepherds tend to these flocks. In the southern part of China is the Plateau of Tibet. To the west of this plateau is the Gobi Desert. North of the desert are snowcapped mountain peaks.

The Himalaya Mountains separate China from India, Bhutan, and Nepal. Mount Everest, the highest mountain in the world, is one of the peaks of the Himalayas. This mountain is shared by China and the tiny country of Nepal. Many mountain climbers have lost their lives attempting to climb its icy cliffs.

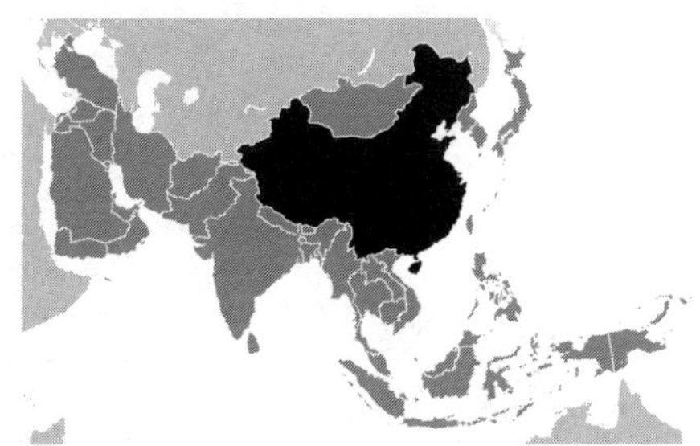

Hong Kong, a peninsula attached to China, consists of more than 200 islands. The British had held Hong Kong as a colony since 1842. In 1997, it was returned to Chinese control by the British. China has agreed to let Hong Kong keep its current **capitalist** economy for the next 50 years. Over the years, many Chinese from the mainland have fled to Hong Kong to escape wars or **invasions** by foreign countries. More than 6 million people, mostly Chinese, live in Hong Kong.

Words to Know

capitalist:
a person whose money and property are used in business

invasion:
an act of going beyond ones own boundaries or limits; usually to conquer or plunder another area

moat:
a deep, wide ditch, often filled with water; may be found around a fortress or castle

textile:
a woven or knitted cloth material

Tibet

The Communist Party took control of China in 1949, after World War II. In 1950 Chinese troops invaded the country of Tibet, in central Asia. The Communist Chinese insisted that Tibet was part of Chinese territory.

In the years that followed, China persecuted the inhabitants of Tibet and their culture. Today there are many organizations devoted to freeing Tibet from Chinese rule and letting the Tibetans decide their own future.

LESSON REVIEW

Directions: Number your paper from 1 to 5. Then answer the following questions.

1. In which section of China do most people live? Why?
2. What natural resources are found on the Manchurian Plain?
3. Why is the Chang considered China's most important river?
4. What is a typhoon?
5. Why was the Great Wall of China built?

LESSON 2: Life in the Cities of China

Most people in China live in villages and small towns. About a hundred cities in China have populations of more than a million people. Nearly all of China's large cities are in the eastern part of the country. Some of these cities are thousands of years old. Ancient walls, towers, and gates still stand as reminders of the past.

China's cities have been changing in recent years. Many have modern factories, steel mills, shipyards, apartment houses, and large department stores. Industry is important to China; it provides many jobs. The country produces a variety of goods including steel, chemicals, farm machinery, and **textiles**. Many of these factories are in Shanghai, the largest city in China. Other important industrial cities are Beijing, Guangzhou, and Tientsin.

Beijing has been the capital city of China for more than 700 years. It has always been considered the center of the Chinese universe. The oldest part of the city is called the Forbidden City. It is sealed off by a wall and a **moat**. Here tourists can see where the emperors lived in ancient times, separated from the rest of the people. Tourists can also visit modern places, such as the Great Hall of the People and Chairman Mao's Museum. Tiananmen Square is the heart of modern Beijing.

The Forbidden City is a popular tourist attraction.

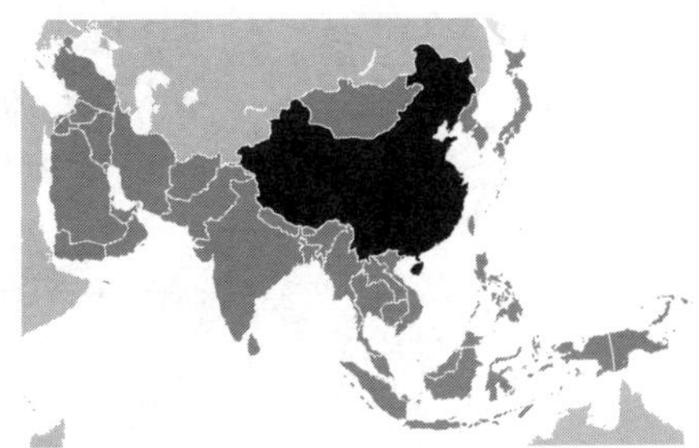

Chapter 3 – China

Words to Know

brocade:
a type of cloth with woven designs

complex:
a group of related or connected buildings

consumer :
a person who buys and uses food or products

enterprise:
a business organization

sampan:
a small, flat-bottomed boat

Shanghai is located at the mouth of the Chang River. (The Chang Zhang is also called the Yangtse River.) It is a busy seaport. The largest city in China, it has a population of 13 million people. Today Shanghai is the site of many new office buildings and roads. Sometimes whole neighborhoods are torn down to make way for the new construction. The streets of the downtown area are very crowded, and vehicles of all types fill the streets. The economic crisis of the late 1990s did affect growth in Shanghai. But recently, the opening of new businesses has created more jobs.

Guangzhou is in southern China on the Xi River. It is the site of large trade fairs. People from all over the world meet here to do business with the Chinese. Guangzhou is also a city of canals. The **sampans** can be seen on these canals.

Changsha, Zhuzhou, and Shaoshan are three cities that make up a large industrial **complex** known as Wuhan. These cities are located southwest of Shanghai on the Chang Zhang. In and around these cities are many industries and railroad yards. In Changsha, many people live in crowded, two-story wooden shacks.

Three other cities of China are noted for their beauty. Nanjing is on the Chang River and has a beautiful double-decker bridge built over the river. The bridge carries traffic on the upper deck, and the trains travel below. Suzhou is a city of lakes and ponds connected by canals. It was a favorite city of the emperors because of its charming and peaceful gardens. Hangzhou is west of Shanghai and is on West Lake. Three islands on the lake provide gardens, a museum, and a library. The city is famous for its silk industry and the beautiful **brocades** it produces.

This ancient temple stands as a reminder of China's past.

Neighborhoods

Factory workers live either in the older neighborhoods or in apartment houses. Some of the apartments are built by the government, and others are built by the factory owners. Most of the apartments have modern conveniences, but the rooms are very small. Sometimes, more than one family must share an apartment.

Each apartment complex or neighborhood is supervised by a committee that is made up of people who live in the community. The committee organizes special programs for the residents. Some of these programs include day care and afternoon activities for children. The committee organizes night classes for the adults. The committee also deals with any small crimes that may occur.

Private Businesses

Between 1978 and 1982, private businesses grew rapidly in the cities. The state decided to allow private businesses to exist to produce more taxes for the government. By 1984 there were 3.25 million people in private **enterprises**. Some of these businesses include restaurants, repair shops, tailor shops, clothing stores, food stores, and flower shops. There are also many jobs for cooks, nannies, and maids in the cities. People who are earning more money are demanding **consumer** goods. They want radios, televisions, and Western-style clothing, especially blue jeans. Not enough of these goods are produced to satisfy everyone. As a result, crime is increasing in the cities. Smugglers are bringing in illegal goods to sell at high prices. Stealing is also increasing.

LESSON REVIEW

Directions: Number your paper from 1 to 6. Then answer the following questions.

1. In what part of the country are most Chinese cities located?
2. What famous square is located in Beijing?
3. What is the older part of Beijing called?
4. What is China's largest city? Why is it important?
5. Why are both Nanjing and Hangzhou noted for their beauty?
6. What reason is given for the increase in crime in China's cities?

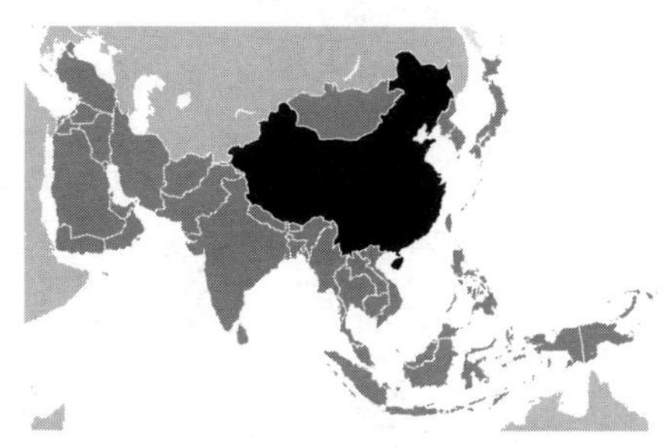

Words to Know

corrupt:
dishonest; evil or wicked

diplomatic relations:
cooperation between countries that makes it possible to trade with each other

prehistoric:
describing a time before historical events were recorded or written down

LESSON 3: The History and Contributions of China

Powerful dynasties ruled China until the early 1900s. This unique governing system developed from civilizations and cultures dating back to **prehistoric** times. The first dynasty, known as the Shang dynasty, was established during the 1700s B.C. The Manchus, the last dynasty, were in power until the early 1900s.

The Chinese people made important contributions to civilization during this time. The invention of paper and a system of writing are both credited to the ancient Chinese. Art, education, and philosophy were developed. The Chinese also invented gunpowder, the compass, movable type for printing, and the method for making hard-glazed porcelain.

The fall of the dynasty structure began as early as the end of the eighteenth century. Government **corruption**, wars, and warfare against the government by the people made the Manchu dynasty weak.

During the nineteenth century, British merchants began bringing Indian-grown opium, a drug, to China. They wanted to balance their trade with China, who exported more than it imported. This conflict led to the Opium War, won by Great Britain in 1842. China and Great Britain signed a treaty that weakened China because it gave the colony of Hong Kong to Great Britain. Unrest and warfare occurred between China and other countries. A short war with Japan between 1894 and 1895 made China accept Japan's control of Korea and give the island of Taiwan to Japan. Secret societies made up of rebels threatened the already weakened government. The Manchus tried to reorganize the Chinese government and economy.

The United League was formed from a number of revolutionary groups. Through its efforts, the provinces in south and central China became independent from the Manchus. By 1912 the Nationalist Party was established.

The philosophy of the people of China began to change. Communism, supported by the Soviet Union, was beginning to be organized in large cities. A conflict arose between the Communists and the Nationalists. The Nationalists were weakened because of their participation in World War II. The capital city of Peking (now Beijing) collapsed into Communist hands in 1949. The Nationalists then set up their government on the nearby island of Taiwan.

The Communists named the nation the People's Republic of China. Mao Zedong became the party chairman, and Chou En-lai was the premier. From 1949 to 1970, the country was closed to the outside world.

China and the Rest of the World

Diplomatic relations with Western countries began to change during the 1970s. U.S. President Richard Nixon visited China in 1972. This friendly gesture toward China improved relations, since there had been no official contact since the Communist takeover. The visit resulted in the signing of the Shanghai Communiqué that established normal relations between China and the United States.

Mao Zedong and Chou En-lai both died in 1976. By 1977 Deng Xiaoping, a moderate, was named vice-chairman of the Communist Party. Another moderate who took office at this time was Hu Yaobang. He was criticized because he agreed with the demands for more rights by Chinese students and others. He was eventually removed from office and died in April of 1989.

China began to seek friendly relations with Western world countries, including the United States. Shortly after Yaobang's death, however, students from some of China's colleges and universities began to demand freedom and democracy. They gathered in Tiananmen Square. The Chinese leaders sent soldiers to break up the demonstrators. These soldiers fired at the students who refused to leave. Many people were killed or arrested. The entire world was shocked at the brutality the Chinese government used in dealing with these students.

LESSON REVIEW

Directions: Number your paper from 1 to 5. Then answer the following questions.

1. Name five inventions credited to the Chinese during the dynasty period.
2. What did the Communists name China?
3. What was the result of President Nixon's visit to China in 1972?
4. Why do you think the student demonstrations took place so soon after Hu Yaobang's death?
5. Do you think China will ever become a democratic country? Explain your answer.

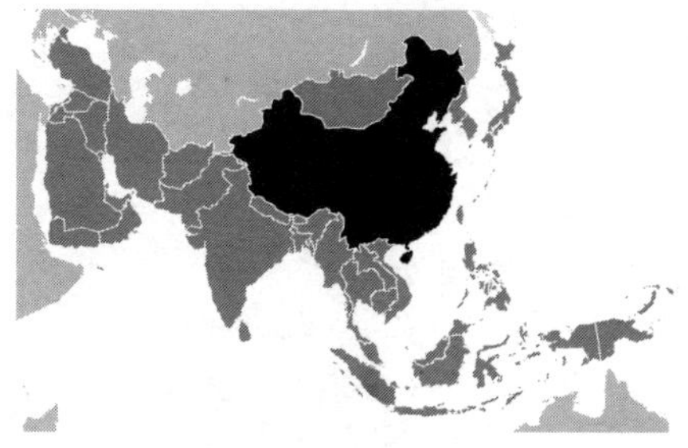

LESSON 4: The Government of China

The official name of the country is People's Republic of China. It is the largest country in the world, with more than 1 billion people. For the last 50 years, it has been controlled by the Communist Party. There are some non-Communist parties, but they have little power.

The People's Liberation Army (PLA) is the military branch of the Communist Party. Most of the citizens of China have supported the government from the beginning. In the past, China's leaders controlled everything that was written in newspapers and magazines. Today, freedom of speech has expanded in China.

China is a Socialist country. This means the government plays an important role in the economy. In industry, the government sets the prices and wage limits and decides were products can be sold. The government also controls most foreign trade.

The Great Wall of China is the only architectural structure that can be seen from space.

Local Governments

The vast country of China is divided into provinces, much like the United States is divided into states. The provinces have their own leaders and other officials. In the past, China's government had complete authority over these provinces. Today, the leaders of the provinces have more control. The Communist Party allows the provinces to take care of their own economy, but it still keeps close watch on them.

Aside from the provinces, there are also five independent regions located in the western areas of the country. The regions were originally set up for the minority people; that is, those who were not Han Chinese. They were once allowed to run their own affairs, but now they are under the rule of the Communist Party. The leaders in these areas still try to preserve the special culture and interests of the ethnic groups that live within their borders.

LESSON REVIEW

Directions: Number your paper from 1 to 4. Then answer the following questions.

1. What is the PLA?
2. What does it mean to be a Socialist country?
3. What do the provinces have control of in their region?
4. Why were the five independent regions set up?

Medical Practices

The Chinese practice a combination of traditional and Western-style medicine. Traditional Chinese medicine includes the use of herbs and an ancient technique called acupuncture. In acupuncture, doctors use a series of needles to stimulate certain reactions in the body. The method is used to treat such things as arthritis and some internal diseases.

The Chinese have adopted many of the drugs and surgical practices from the West. Modern medical care has been made available to many more Chinese through clinics and hospitals. Clinics that are staffed by part-time medical workers have been set up in small country villages. These medical workers, called barefoot doctors, are mostly women. They treat simple illnesses, vaccinate people against diseases, check the purity of the drinking water, and give advice on infant care and nutrition. Most medical bills are paid by the state.

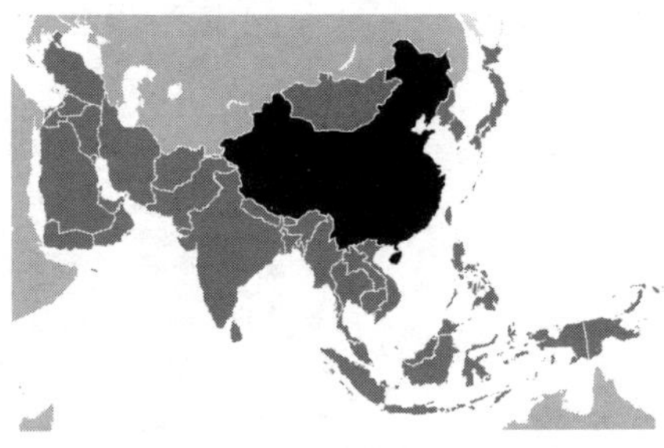

Words to Know

commune:
a group of people living and working together; all property is owned by the group

cooperative:
an organization owned by and operated for the benefit of those using its services

nomad:
a person who wanders searching for food and/or pasture land

LESSON 5: The People of China

China has the largest population in the world—over one billion people. In the past, Chinese families were very large. Today the government encourages families to have fewer children, because of limited resources in the country. In some cities, couples who promise to have only one child are given money each month until the child is 14 years old. Sometimes, other rewards are offered to these small families, such as better jobs, nicer housing, and entrance into the best schools.

The Han Chinese people live mainly in the eastern part of the country. All the Han Chinese share the same culture, language, history, and customs. Most of them are farmers. Their ancestors have been living in China for thousands of years.

The rest of China's population is made up of minority groups. The Mongol people are the largest minority group, with about two million people living in a dry and desolate region of western China. The Mongols are wandering **nomads** who live by tending herds of sheep, cattle, camels, or horses.

The Tibetans are another minority group. They make their home on the lovely Plateau of Tibet that is 16,000 feet above sea level. Their homeland is called the "roof of the world." The majestic, snow-capped Himalaya Mountains surround this plateau.

Family Life

In the past Chinese society stressed family life, with all members of the family working together. The eldest male ruled their family even if the entire family could not live together. Children and women were obedient to the men. Marriages were arranged for the young people, and women did not work outside the home. Today, family units are much smaller, and the women and children have more freedom.

The Chinese make their own clothing out of cotton or a synthetic fabric. Both men and women wear clothes similar to those worn by people in the Western nations. Adults usually wear dull colors. Only children and young women wear brightly colored clothing. Hair styles are also changing, but many women still wear their hair in simple styles.

Some minority groups speak the language and follow the customs of the Han Chinese. Other groups speak their own language and have their own customs. The Han Chinese have often looked down on these small minority groups. In the past, the Han have tried to force the minority groups to speak their language and follow their way of living.

People on the Farm

More than half of the people in China are farmers. This figure is much higher than the number of farmers in the United States. Before 1949 many Chinese farmers owned their own land. When the Communists took over these farms, farmers lost their land. Other private property was also seized during the 1950s.

The farmers and peasants were then organized into farm **communes**. Large farms were made up of farmers who lived and worked together as a society. They had common ownership of the land, tools, work animals, and small factories. The workers of the commune were organized into production teams, each with a different job to perform. Each commune family was allowed to keep a share of the crops they grew.

In the late 1970s, the government changed many of the farm communes into farm **cooperatives**. A farm cooperative is a group of farm families or households who work together but earn their own money. This new system has been successful in most areas of China. Many different crops are now grown in the new system. Recently, farmers were given the right to contract for the land they will farm. They now have greater freedom in what crops they grow. They can now sell their excess crops in a free market.

The government hoped that by organizing cooperatives, grain production would be increased if households worked for themselves. The households on farm cooperatives are required to give part of their grain to the state. In reality, the amount of grain produced has decreased since cooperatives were formed. The farmers have discovered that they can make more money by growing and selling other crops besides grain. Therefore, the farmer only grows the amount of grain required to give to the government. The result is that there is not enough grain to feed the millions of Chinese people.

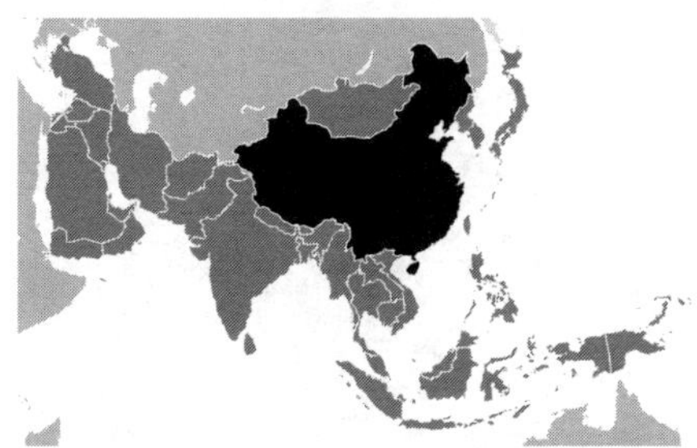

This Chinese family is at home in Chengdu, Szechwan.

People in Rural Areas

Rural people can own their own houses although the land still belongs to the state. The farm cooperatives have made it possible for farmers to afford new houses. These houses are usually made of mud and clay bricks. They have two or three bedrooms, and the roof is made of straw. A special feature of some homes is the *kang*, a long brick platform with a space underneath. It is connected to the kitchen oven. Hot air flows through the space on the way to the chimney and heats the platform. In very cold weather, some family members wrap in blankets and sleep on the platform. The wealthier villages have apartment houses.

What do village people do for recreation? Some villages and neighborhoods have recreation areas where movies are shown weekly. Libraries also offer classes in reading and writing. Table tennis and basketball are very popular sports.

LESSON REVIEW

Directions: Number your paper from 1 to 5. Then answer the following questions.

1. What minority groups live in China?
2. How do the Mongol people earn their living?
3. What is a farm cooperative?
4. What is another name for the Plateau of Tibet?
5. What are farmers' houses made out of?

Chapter 3 – China

The Chu Family

In the large cities of China, many families have only one or two children. The Chu family has three family members: *Hsou Lan Chu* (the mother), *Chun Chu* (the father), and *Zhi Ke Chu* (the daughter).

The Chus live in Guangzhou in southern China. Their apartment is in a large complex owned by the city. It has four small rooms—kitchen, living room, bedroom, and bathroom. Both Mr. and Mrs. Chu work six days a week at a nearby factory that makes heavy machinery. Hsou Lan is in charge of the ordering department. Chun runs a machine that makes gears. Each day, on the way home from work, Hsou Lan stops at the market to buy the groceries. They share the household chores and the cooking. On their day off, they sometimes visit a museum or a park.

Zhi attends school six days a week. She studies math, history, politics, and geography; she also enjoys gymnastics. At home she helps with the chores, does her own laundry, and spends two or three hours doing homework each night. In the future Zhi hopes to go to college.

The Temple Street Night Market is in Kowloon, Hong Kong.

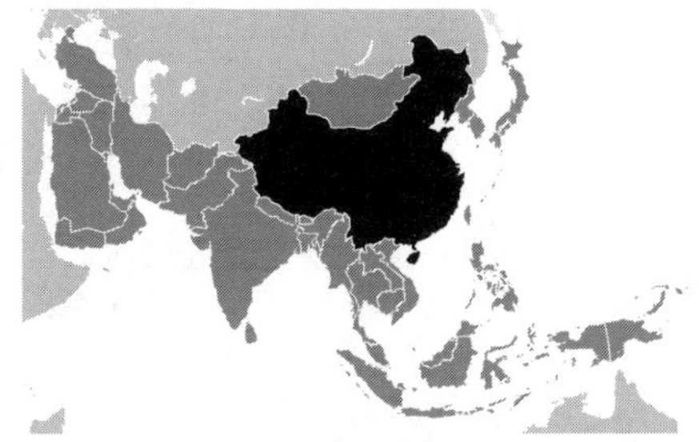

LESSON 6: China Is Changing

After China's leader Mao Zedong died in 1976, the new leaders made many changes. They believed that more food, industries, and consumer goods were needed. They made many changes to allow the Chinese people to make more money. Two of these changes included changing farm communes to cooperatives and allowing people to become self-employed.

In one area of China, the Sichuan province, changes were made very quickly. In the busy city of Chengdu, many people wear Western-style sweaters and jeans. They shop in privately owned shops that sell a variety of goods including televisions, radios, tapes, and American movie magazines. Tourists are welcomed in this city. The people are friendly and eager to learn from foreigners about life outside China.

The Railroad System Is Changing People's Lives

Another change in the Chinese people's way of life concerns travel, especially by railroad. Since 1949 a national rail system has been a major goal of the government. In recent years, thousands of miles of track have been added to the railway system. The Chinese people are allowed to travel without applying for a government pass, which they needed in the past. Salesmen, students, families visiting relatives, and people touring the country use the new railroad. Chinese and foreigners alike have discovered that the railway is the best way to travel through China because of the badly paved highways.

Modern-day Beijing is a bustling city.

Now China is one of the world's major railroad builders. However, the rugged land and mountains make building railroads very difficult. More than 400 tunnels and bridges have been built along the tracks. Steam engines are used in most places because China has a large amount of coal. Some electric trains have been used in recent years.

Religions Are Returning to China

A religion called Taoism was started in China about 200 B.C. Taoists believed in a simpler way of life than the Confucianists practiced. They believed that man could find real peace if he lived in harmony with nature and the universe. Taoism was a religion of many gods to whom the people prayed for protection in troubled times. Before a.d. 100, the Buddhist religion came to China from India. Chinese Buddhism was influenced by some beliefs of Confucianism and Taoism.

In the United States and Canada, people have the right to practice any religion they choose. Americans are guaranteed this right by the Constitution. But after the Communist takeover in China in 1949, the Chinese people were forbidden to practice religion of any kind. They were encouraged to study and practice only Communist ideas. Even the teachings of Confucius, which had influenced Chinese culture for centuries, were forbidden by the government.

During the 1970s, the government changed its mind and gradually began allowing people to practice their religions. Places of worship that had been closed or turned into warehouses and museums were reopened. Many of the beautiful temples were restored. The ideas of Confucius are being read and taught once again.

The number of Chinese Christians has increased in recent years. But Chinese leaders still forbid worship that is not approved by the state. They forbid foreign religious workers from handing out Bibles. In some parts of China, police persecution of Christians is common.

Education in China

In China most young children start their education in day-care centers because both parents usually work. When children are six or seven, they enter elementary school. Learning to read and write the Chinese language is difficult. Chinese children do not learn the 26 letters of the alphabet as English-speaking children do. Children in China learn characters, or symbols, that represent words. In the first two years of school they must learn over 800 characters. By the third year of school, they are expected to know more than 3,000 characters!

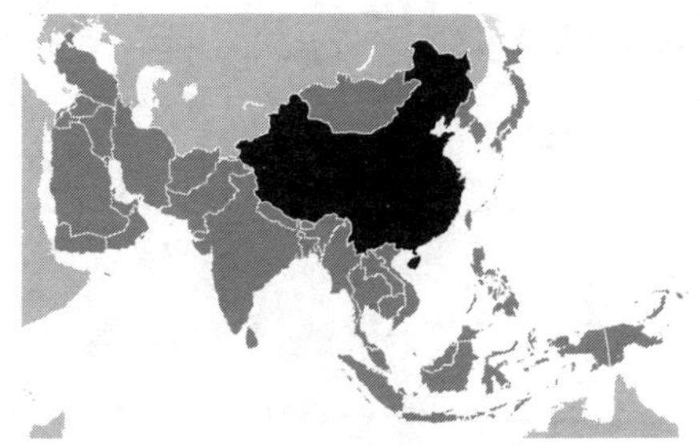

Most of the other subjects taught in Chinese schools are the same as those taught in American schools. Political science, an important school subject, is taught even in elementary school. Physical fitness is important. Gymnastics is very popular with both boys and girls.

After elementary school, children attend middle school for about three years. Part of every school day is set aside for sports such as basketball, table tennis, wrestling, or boxing.

China does not have enough universities for every student to attend. A student must pass an exam to enter a university. Even if a student passes an exam, he or she may not be able to enroll because the schools are overcrowded. The university teaches languages, economics, and social sciences. Technical schools are for students who want to study medicine or teaching. These technical schools also offer courses in agriculture, forestry, and mining. Factories also provide classes for people to learn the skills needed in industry. However, they do not have enough trained people to run and manage the many factories. Thousands of young Chinese are sent to other countries for technical training and education. The government sends these students to Japan, Europe, and the United States. When they return, they teach the Chinese workers what they have learned.

LESSON REVIEW

Directions: Number your paper from 1 to 5. Then answer the following questions.

1. Name two changes that occurred after the death of Mao Zedong.
2. Why has travel by rail become popular in recent years?
3. Why were religious practices banned in China?
4. Why do you think the Chinese government is allowing people to now practice their religions?
5. Why are some young Chinese being sent out of the country for technical education? Do you think that this practice will continue?

LESSON 7: Recreation, Holidays, and Festivals

Festivals and holidays have always been important to the Chinese. These occasions usually mark the changing of seasons, show respect for old customs, or celebrate important political events.

One of the most important festivals for the Chinese is the Chinese New Year. It is primarily a time for visiting with friends and relatives. But, it is also a time for clearing debts and buying new clothes. The main shopping areas are decorated with colorful banners and lights. Neighborhood associations plan their own special activities. The Chinese Feast of Lanterns officially marks the end of the Chinese New Year celebration. During this happy time, huge paper dragons, firecrackers, and lanterns are displayed. The cold northeastern province of Harbin holds an Ice Lantern Festival. Structures are carved from ice, and colored lanterns are placed inside. A favorite spring holiday includes visiting the graves of ancestors. Other holidays are International Working Women's Day and People's Liberation Army Day.

Spectators enjoy a martial arts show in Beijing.

The Arts

Many works of ancient Chinese literature teach a moral lesson or express a religious or political idea. The ancient Chinese philosopher, Confucius, was a very important writer. His works were widely read and his ideas followed until the 1900s. Other important writers were various Buddhists or Taoists, who also wrote about religious ideas. Poetry has always been popular in China. Poems were written about friendship, love, and nature. In ancient China, writers and poets were honored and usually held high government positions.

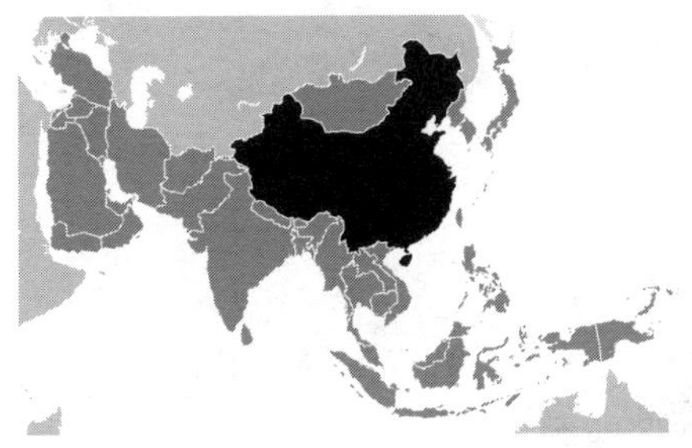

Words to Know

convert:
to change

In the late 1800s, writings began to tell about problems in society. After the rise of communism, literature was used to teach people about the Communist Party and the good it was doing for the people of China. During this time traditional arts such as drama, ballet, and opera were replaced by new opera-ballets that were written to teach a political lesson. Most of these new opera-ballets ended with everyone being **converted** to communism. In 1972 when President Nixon visited China, he saw one of these opera-ballets performed. Since the death of Mao Zedong in 1976, the traditional style operas, ballets, and dramas are being performed again. The famous Beijing Opera consists of music, acting, dancing, and acrobatics. The actors wear elaborate costumes and color their faces. These operas are performed with very little scenery.

Painting, Sculpture, and Ceramics

The Chinese have been making beautiful pottery and statues for thousands of years. When scientists dug up the tombs and cities of the ancient Chinese, thousands of bronze statues and clay and ceramic vessels were uncovered. Many of these ceramics had colored glazes. Others were decorated with dragons or beasts. Some were made of a fine porcelain. The Chinese were the first to make porcelain, which is a thin yet hard type of ceramic. Chinese porcelain has always been popular throughout the world.

These terra cotta soldiers are some of the 8,000 figures in the Qin pottery army. They were discovered in the tomb of an emperor who lived more than 2,000 years ago.

Landscape painting was closely related to religion and philosophy. It was the most popular form of painting. Most paintings were in black and white with large areas left unpainted. The artists felt this openness made pictures more beautiful. Figures, buildings, or boats were painted against a background of mountains, pine trees, or water. Most paintings were done on scrolls and rolled up when not on display. Poems or verses, written in elegant handwriting, were often included on the paintings.

Architecture

Chinese architecture usually features a courtyard enclosed by buildings. The most outstanding feature of these buildings is a large tile roof with edges that extend out and curve up. Typical of this type of architecture is the Forbidden City in Beijing, the former home of the emperors. The ancient cities of China were laid out like a chessboard with important government buildings facing north and south. China is also famous for stone arch bridges. Gardens have been constructed since ancient times. They include waterfalls, pools, statues, and pavilions. The largest project of the ancient Chinese was the Great Wall, which stretches for 1,400 miles.

Symbols of nature are often used to decorate works of art. The plum blossom stands for courage and hope; geese are a symbol of happy married life; and the tiger is a symbol of energy and strength. One of the most important symbols is a dragon. The dragon means many things to the Chinese: an emperor, a sign of the zodiac, or a hero in a folktale.

LESSON REVIEW

Directions: Number your paper from 1 to 4. Then answer the following questions.

1. What is the most important Chinese holiday? How do the people celebrate it?
2. What was discovered when scientists dug up ancient Chinese cities and tombs?
3. The dragon is an important symbol. How is it used in architecture and art? How is it used during festivals and celebrations?
4. After the rise of communism, why do you think that traditional Chinese literature, drama, ballet, and opera were ignored?

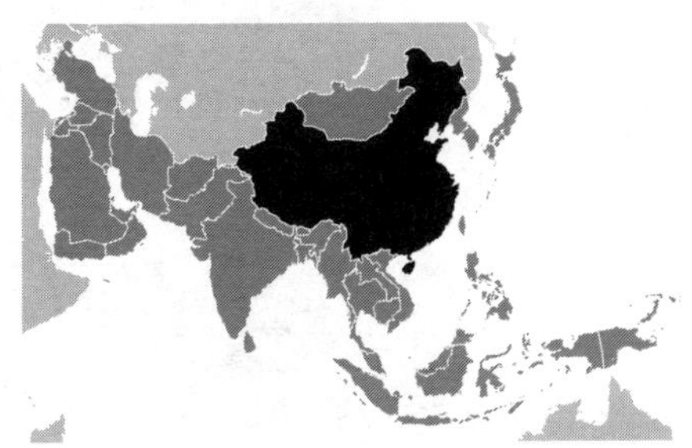

Spotlight Story

Cooking Chinese Style

The Chinese consider eating to be one of the joys of life. The teachings and philosophies of Confucius and Taoism had an effect on the way they traditionally prepared their food. They believe that foods should blend together to create a pleasing taste. The taste comes from these blends—sweet and sour, hot and cold, salty and bland, or smooth and crunchy. The good nutrition of proper foods is recognized as the means to a long and happy life.

The preparation of Chinese food requires great care. Food is cut into small pieces so it cooks quickly. Often the meat is marinated to improve the flavor. Pork, beef, duck, fish, and chicken are the main meats. Seasonings include ginger, sesame seeds, and soy sauce. Rice is the grain most often used in the south; in the north they use wheat. A wide assortment of vegetables and fruits such as pineapple, raisins, cherries, and oranges are also used.

There are five main methods of preparing Chinese food—sautéing, braising or stewing, deep-frying, steaming, and roasting. Sautéing is the most widely used method of cooking. A large skillet or wok is used. The foods are constantly stirred as they cook.

You probably have eaten and enjoyed Chinese food. There are many Chinese restaurants in our country. You may think Chinese food is difficult to prepare at home, but it is not. Many dishes use only one or two ingredients. If you use the sautéing method, cooking time is very short.

Try the following recipe with your family or friends. Be sure to eat with chopsticks and serve hot tea.

Ssu Chi Niu Ju (Beef with Green Beans)

Ingredients:
1/2 pound thinly sliced beef
1/2 pound fresh green beans
1-1/2 cups boiling water
2 T. cooking oil

Marinade:
2 T. soy sauce
1 T. each sugar, cornstarch, salt

Directions: Mix ingredients for marinade together in a shallow dish. Soak beef in marinade for 20 minutes. Cut beans into 2" lengths, pour boiling water over them, and drain. Save 1/2 cup of the water. Heat oil in a large skillet (or wok) and sauté beef for 20 seconds. Stir constantly. Add beans and stir for another 30 seconds. Add the 1/2 cup water and simmer (cook slowly) for one minute. Serve immediately with cooked rice.

SPOTLIGHT REVIEW

Answer the following questions.

1. Why do the Chinese believe that good nutrition is important?
2. What are some favorite seasonings used in Chinese cooking?
3. What is the most widely used method of Chinese cooking?

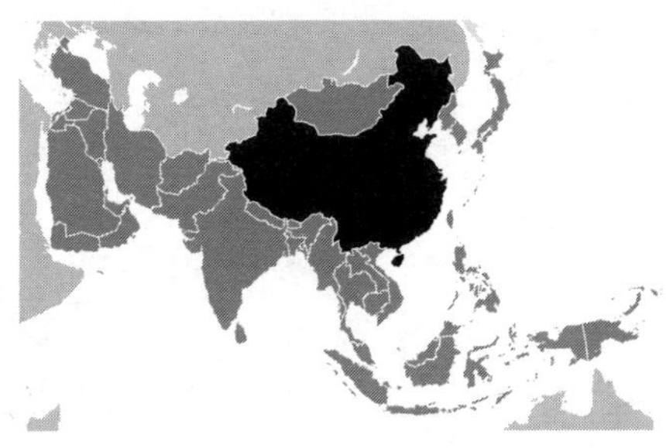

Chapter 3 Review

China has the largest population in the world. The Himalaya Mountains separate China from India, Bhutan, and Nepal. The highest mountain in the world, Mount Everest, is in the Himalayas. The ancient Forbidden City is in Beijing, the capital city of China. Three out of four people in China are farmers.

China was ruled by dynasties until the early 1900s. During this time the Chinese people made many important contributions to civilization. China became a republic when the last dynasty failed. The government has been ruled by the Communist Party since 1949. After Mao Zedong died in 1976, the new leaders made many changes.

Most Chinese look forward to holidays and festivals. Chinese school children and others enjoy many sports. The arts have always been important in China. The country is famous for its beautiful porcelain and landscape painting. In literature, the works of Confucius are known throughout the world.

This summer palace in Beijing, China, overlooks Kunming Lake.

CHAPTER 3 – CHINA

Critical Thinking Skills

Directions: Give some thought to the questions below. Be sure to answer in complete sentences.

1. If you travel on the Chang River in China, what are some sights that you would see?
2. If the Chinese government continues to allow people more freedoms, what do you think will happen to private business?
3. If a young Chinese person left a rural area to find work in a big city, what type of jobs might be available to him or her? What would living conditions be like in a Chinese city?
4. If a Chinese farmer came to the United States to farm, what differences would you tell him to expect in farm organization methods?
5. If you visited China during the celebration of the Chinese New Year, what would you see the people doing during this celebration?

For Discussion

1. Why do you think that the Chinese Communist government took away all private property after 1949?
2. Which invention of the ancient Chinese do you think contributed the most to the development of civilization? Explain your answer.
3. The chapter tells about some changes that have taken place in China. What other changes do you think will take place in the future? Explain your answer.
4. Discuss some basic human rights that you enjoy as a citizen of Canada or the United States. Explain if these same rights are enjoyed by Chinese citizens.
5. Do you think there will be future protest demonstrations by Chinese citizens? Explain your answer.

Write It!

Directions: Write a short paragraph describing one of the following: Great Wall, Beijing, China's Communist Party, acupuncture, or the Chinese railway system. Use books or encyclopedias to find additional information.

For You to Do

Directions: The giant panda is considered a Chinese treasure. Use the library and other sources to write a report describing why pandas are in danger. Explain what is being done to save the pandas.

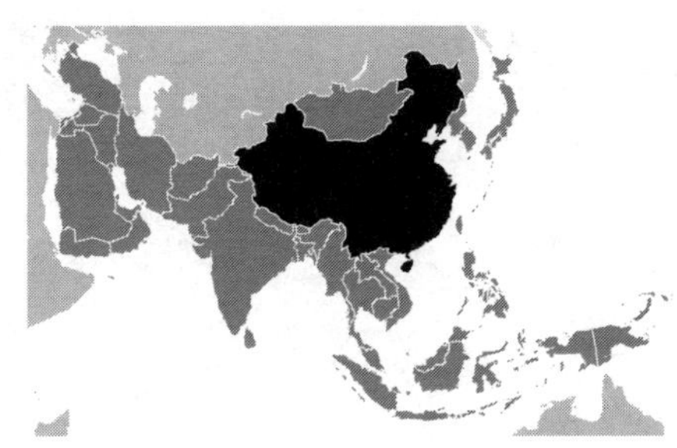

TAIWAN

CHAPTER 4

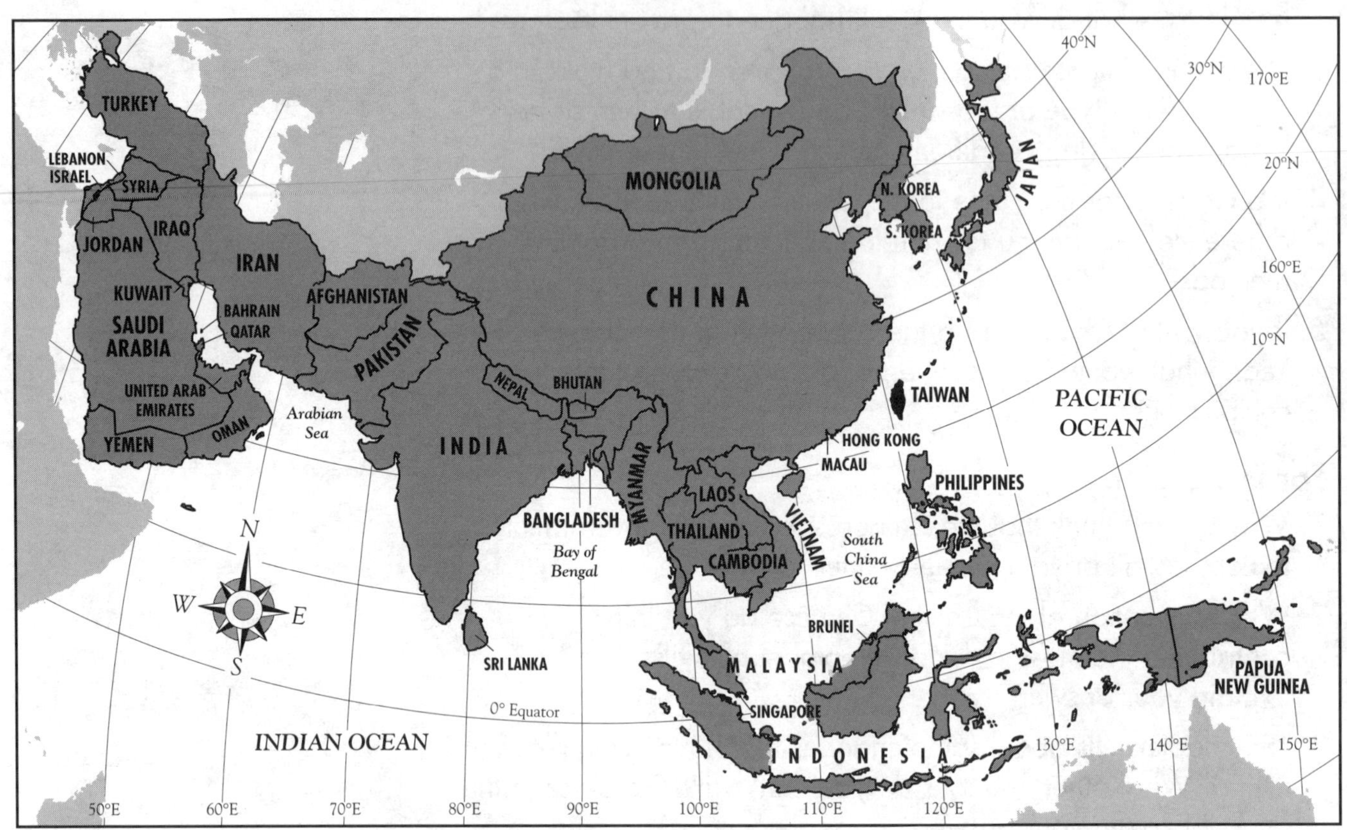

Fast Facts

- The Republic of China, known as Taiwan, is made up of several islands.
- Taiwan's climate is tropical and subtropical. Summers are hot and humid, and winters are mild.
- Taiwan has a democratic government with officials elected by the people.
- There are thousands of Little League teams in Taiwan.

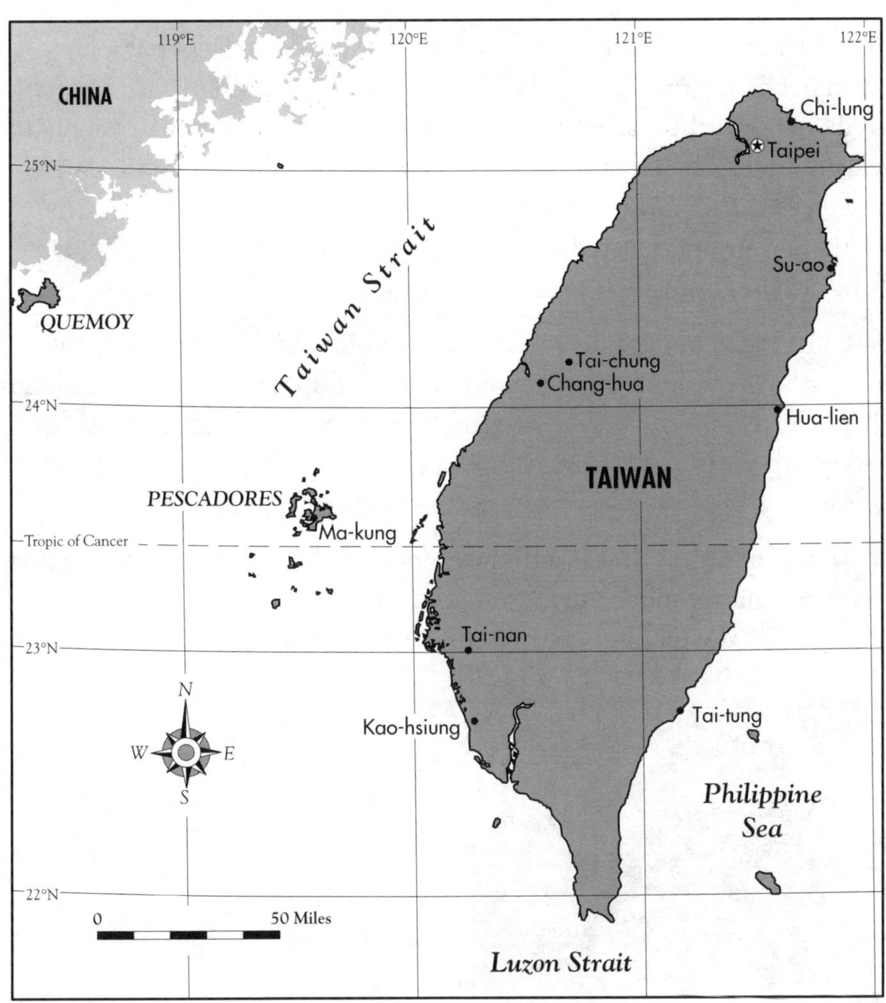

MAP SKILLS

Taiwan

Directions: Study the map above to answer these questions.

1. What country lies northwest of Taiwan?
2. What strait is south of Taiwan?
3. What is the capital of Taiwan?
4. What sea is east of Taiwan?
5. What strait lies between Taiwan and China?

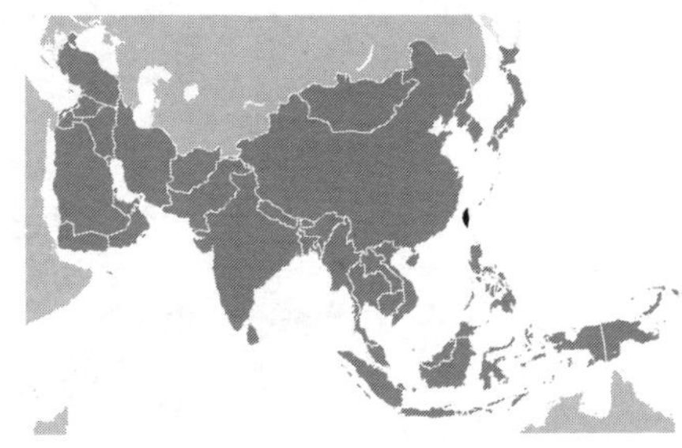

Chapter 4 – Taiwan

Words to Know

civil war:
a war between opposing groups of citizens of one nation

developing country:
a country that is slowly developing its industry and economy

islet:
a little island

LESSON 1: A Look at Taiwan

Today when people speak of Taiwan, they mean the Republic of China. The country has existed since 1949. That's when there was a **civil war**, and the Communist Chinese forced some Chinese people to leave China. These Nationalist Chinese people left mainland China and crossed the Taiwan Strait to start their own government on the island of Taiwan. South Taiwan is the cultural center of the island. When the Chinese first came to Taiwan in 1949, they settled here.

The land now under control of the Republic of China includes the main island of Taiwan. The capital city of Taipei is here. Other islands that are part of the country are the Pescadores and Matsu Islands in the South China Sea, Green Island and Orchid Island on the Pacific Coast, and the Taioyutai **Islets** to the northeast of Taiwan.

Taiwan is a nation that is still developing. It has changed from a poor, backward nation under strict rule to a wealthy, modern democracy. Many other **developing countries** look to Taiwan as a model.

This outdoor market in Taiwan sells fresh chickens.

LESSON REVIEW

Directions: Number your paper from 1 to 4. Then answer the following questions.

1. Since what year has Taiwan existed?
2. What is the capital of Taiwan?
3. What caused some Chinese people to start their own government on Taiwan?
4. What part of the island is the cultural center?

LESSON 2: The Geography of Taiwan

Taiwan is 240 miles long. Two-thirds of the island is covered with mountains that have forests on top. The island is divided north to south by the Chungyang Mountains, which have more than 200 snow-capped peaks. Jade Mountain (also called Yu Shan), the highest peak, is also the tallest peak in all of northeast Asia. East of the Chungyang Mountains the land is rugged, ending in cliffs at the Pacific Ocean. To the west and south the mountains gently slope to plateaus and then become broad, fertile plains. Most people live in this area, and all of the crops are grown here in the rich soil. Only about 10 percent of the region is left for homes and businesses. The capital city of Taipei is located here.

Taiwan's weather is tropical, and typhoons and earthquakes sometimes hit the island.

In northern Taiwan you will find volcanic mountains, historic towns and temples, lakes, waterfalls, and coastal rock formations. This area attracts many visitors. Taiwan's largest campground opened here in 1992. It has modern facilities such as hot showers and electric hookups.

The Chungyang Mountains divide the island of Taiwan from north to south.

LESSON REVIEW

Directions: Number your paper from 1 to 3. Then answer the following questions.

1. Where on Taiwan do most people live? Why do they live there?
2. How long is Taiwan?
3. Where will you find volcanic mountains, with lakes and waterfalls?

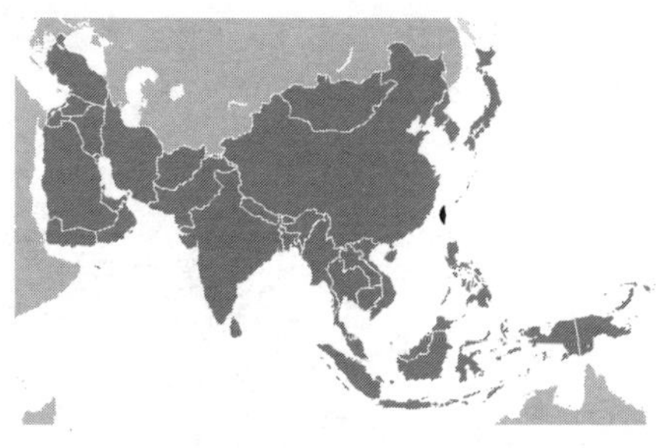

LESSON 3: The History of Taiwan

Taiwan used to be called *Formosa*, which means "beautiful island." It was given this name by the Portuguese sailors who first saw the island in 1590. The Dutch and the Spanish also came in the 1600s. In 1683 the Manchus from mainland China took the island and kept it until 1895. At that time, Japan and China fought a war over Korea. Japan defeated China and was given control of Taiwan. After World War II and the defeat of Japan, Taiwan was given back to China.

In 1946 fighting broke out between the Communist forces and the Nationalist forces, led by Chiang Kai-shek. Both of these armies wanted to control China. The Nationalists lost and went to Taiwan in 1949 to set up their own government there. The Nationalists said that one day they would again control mainland China. This new country, known as Taiwan—Republic of China, was recognized by the United Nations for more than 20 years. But in 1971 the Communist government of the People's Republic of China was admitted to the United Nations. Since only one China could be represented in the United Nations, Taiwan—Republic of China had to leave.

LESSON REVIEW

Directions: Number your paper from 1 to 4. Then answer the following questions.

1. What did Taiwan used to be called?
2. What nationalities visited Taiwan in the 1600s?
3. After World War II, who was Taiwan given back to?
4. When did the Nationalists lose the war with the Communists and go to Taiwan?

LESSON 4: China and Taiwan: An Uneasy Relationship

Since the end of the Chinese civil war in 1949, relations between Taiwan and the People's Republic of China have been tense. When the Nationalists fled to Taiwan and set up their new government, military law was declared. This means that people were not allowed to disagree with the government. This new government was successful, and the economy grew quickly. By 1987 military law was not needed, because the people liked the government. By 1996 the first free presidential elections were held in Taiwan.

Mainland China has remained a one-party state. Changes in the economy did not begin there until 1962. People in China don't make nearly as much money as the people in Taiwan do.

Most people in Taiwan don't want to be part of China again. They like things the way they are. But China wants Taiwan to reunite with them and threatened them by testing missiles near Taiwan.

The people of Taiwan elected a new president, Chen Shui-bian, in March of 2000. This new president would like to keep Taiwan separate from China, but he wants the two countries to be friends. He wants both Taiwan and China to join the World Trade Organization, which would greatly improve the economies of both countries.

This problem of the differences between what the Chinese government wants and what the government of Taiwan wants is a difficult one. The two countries continue to discuss the issue and want to find a peaceful solution.

LESSON REVIEW

Directions: Number your paper from 1 to 3. Then answer the following questions.

1. When were the first free presidential elections held in Taiwan?
2. When was military law no longer needed in Taiwan?
3. Are the governments of Taiwan and the People's Republic of China similar and agreeable?

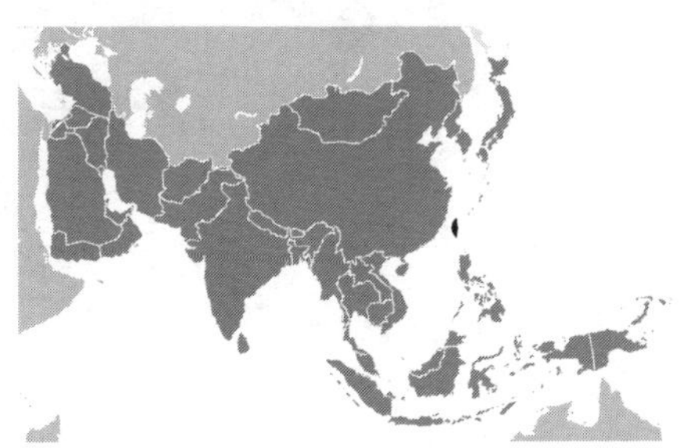

LESSON 5: The Government of Taiwan

Taiwan has had a stable government ever since the country began. It has a democracy, and officials, including the president, are elected by the people. The president then appoints a prime minister, who runs the government.

There have not been any riots or takeovers of the government. This makes the country attractive to foreign investors. In recent years many Taiwanese, including government officials, talk about a separate state for Taiwan. The result would be two separate Chinas.

When there is a political election in Taiwan, most of the country's 22 million people become very excited. Long campaign rallies, or gatherings, are held for each candidate, and sometimes these become very lively. Fireworks are set off, air horns are blasted, and cheering and shouting fill the air. If people cannot attend the rallies, they can watch the events on television.

Long political campaign rallies are popular in Taiwan.

According to the *Liberty Times*, a newspaper in Taiwan, it is common for officials to pay people to vote for a certain candidate. In some areas, this is a tradition.

Voters were excited about the presidential election, because they finally saw a chance to end the 50-year rule of the Kuomintang Party. This political party had been in power since 1949, after being forced from China. The presidential election was held in March of 2000, and the Democratic Progressive Party defeated the Kuomintang Party. Chen Shui-bian became the new president. More than 80 percent of the population turned out to vote. By comparison, in the last presidential election in the United States a little more than 50 percent of the people who were registered to vote turned out to vote.

The Asian Financial Crisis and Taiwan's Economy

In the years before 1998, many Asian countries built factories and started new businesses. Other countries with more money invested in these new businesses and industries.

But in 1998 many Asian countries, including South Korea, Indonesia, and Japan, saw their economies begin to fail. Their businesses closed, and banks stopped loaning money for new industries. Foreign countries stopped lending them money, because they were no longer profiting from their investments.

Taiwan's economy had grown along with the economies of other Asian countries. However, when the other countries began losing money, Taiwan was able to keep its economy steady. This was because Taiwan had received very few loans from foreign countries. Also, Taiwan's banking methods were different from those in other countries. As a result, new companies in Taiwan were able to get loans easily at home. They did not have to ask foreign countries for money.

Many Taiwanese companies also made products for American and Japanese firms and did not manufacture their own brands. By doing this, they avoided the high cost of starting new businesses and paying for advertising, equipment, and workers. In the future, if foreign businesses fail again, Taiwan will adjust by starting new businesses at home.

LESSON REVIEW

Directions: Number your paper from 1 to 4. Then answer the following questions.

1. Who appoints the prime minister?
2. Who elects the president?
3. Who runs the government?
4. How do most people in Taiwan feel about political elections?

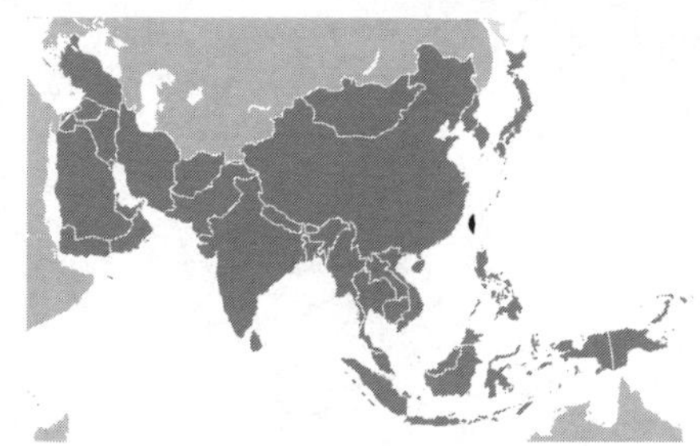

LESSON 6: The Economy of Taiwan

In the 50 years since it was created, Taiwan has made steady progress in all areas, including its economy. This happened even though Taiwan spent a lot of money to keep its military strong. China has threatened many times to use drastic measures to meet the goal of a unified nation that includes Taiwan.

Taiwan is one of the world's top 15 trading nations. Many products made in Taiwan are exported around the world. More than 28 percent of the industry in Taiwan is manufacturing, including information technology and electronics. In 2000, Taiwan's gross national product was $357 billion. A large number of Taiwan's manufacturers have set up factories across the Taiwan Strait in mainland China. Labor and other costs are lower there. Taiwan's business interests have spread to other activities on Mainland China. These include real estate, insurance, banking, and tourism. These are gradually replacing food processing and garment manufacturing as Taiwan's most important industries. Taiwan's forests are its most valuable natural resource.

Taiwan has only a small market for their manufactured goods at home. More than 90 percent of their manufactured goods are exported around the globe. The standard of living of the people of Taiwan is one of the highest in the world. The average income for each person in Taiwan is about $17,000 a year. The yearly income in the United States was $31,500 in the spring of 2000.

LESSON REVIEW

Directions: Number your paper from 1 to 5. For each question, write *T* for true or *F* for false.

1. Taiwan keeps a strong military.
2. Taiwan is not one of the world's top trading nations.
3. Taiwan's manufacturers have set up factories in China.
4. The standard of living is higher in Taiwan than in the United States.
5. Most of Taiwan's products stay in their country.

LESSON 7: The People of Taiwan and Their Culture

The population of Taiwan is more than 22 million, with Taipei and Kaohsiung the most densely populated cities. More than 60 percent of the population lives on the plains and basins west of the Chungyang Mountains.

Most of the people are Han Chinese. The rest of the population are aborigines, descendants of the first inhabitants. There are about 440,000 aborigines in Taiwan and the neighboring islands. The government has worked to improve the lives of the aborigines with medical care, legal services, and vocational training.

All the Han Chinese, both on mainland China and in Taiwan, share the same culture. There is a great emphasis on learning in Taiwan, and the government gives generous amounts of money to education. As a result, the Taiwanese are highly educated and have a high literacy rate. Most citizens of Taiwan value the family and show respect for the government by following the laws.

People in Taiwan often practice tai chi in public parks. Tai chi consists of gentle stretching movements said to help keep a healthy body and calm mind.

LESSON REVIEW

Directions: Number your paper from 1 to 3. Then answer the following questions.

1. What are the two most populated cities in Taiwan?
2. What two groups make up the populations of Taiwan?
3. Is education considered important to the people of Taiwan?

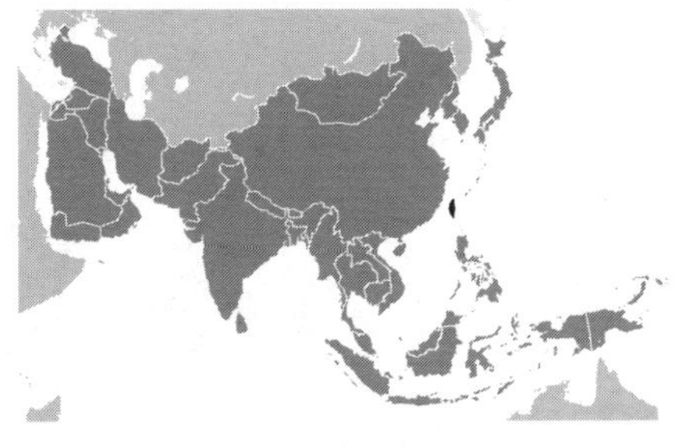

Words to Know

constitutional: according to the constitution, or principles, of a nation

LESSON 8: Education and Religion

The Taiwanese place great importance on education. Preschool is popular now because of the competitive nature of the education system. Difficult entrance examinations are required for all schools beyond ninth grade. Some students will attend a "cram school" at the same time they attend regular school in order to pass the entrance exams for schools after the ninth grade. If they fail the exams, they may then attend the cram school for another full year before taking the exams again. This is the standard way to gain admission to schools.

Taiwan is in the process of reforming its education system. Some educators think there is too much pressure on students trying to enter a school after the ninth grade. They are looking at other ways for students to qualify, such as grades, performance in school, and test scores. Some of these experimental programs began in 1998 and were successful.

After ninth grade, students may choose to attend a senior high school, a vocational school, or a junior college. Only about 6 percent of students drop out of school after ninth grade. Most of the colleges and university programs are four years, except for law and medical programs. Taiwan has about 140 colleges and universities, attended by more than 900,000 students. As the demand for higher education increases, Taiwan is opening more colleges and universities.

Religion in Taiwan

Freedom of religion is a **constitutional** right of every citizen in Taiwan, just as it is in the United States. About half of the people of Taiwan follow folk religion. This religion is a mixture of Buddhist, Confucian, and Taoist rituals and social customs.

The Taoists place great emphasis on freedom and mystical experiences. They follow the writings of Lao-tzu. They believe people who live in harmony with nature will become immortal. Buddhism stresses moral codes and places great emphasis on Buddhist education. Confucianism is based on the writings of Confucius. He was a great teacher and philosopher who gave advice on how to behave in an ethical and moral way. His birthday is cause for great celebration.

The folk religion ceremonies are mixed with other festivals and social events. It is common to see a lighted shrine with burning incense in homes and shops. These may honor a god, hero, or ancestor. Taxi drivers decorate their cars with charms or small statues for protection against accidents.

This man is praying in a Buddhist monastery.

Some Christianity is also practiced in Taiwan, with Presbyterians and Baptists the largest groups.

Religious groups provide many services for the population. They operate hospitals, clinics, retirement homes, centers for children with special needs, and orphanages. They share a common concern for the poor or unfortunate. Churches also lead in organizing cultural events and recreational activities. Presbyterians promote activities for youths. Taoists organize and present traditional Chinese dramas, while the Buddhists offer a wide range of self-improvement methods.

LESSON REVIEW

Directions: Number your paper from 1 to 5. Then answer the following questions.

1. What kind of school can students attend to help them pass the exams for entrance into schools after ninth grade?
2. What kinds of schools can students attend after ninth grade?
3. Do many students drop out of school after ninth grade?
4. Folk religion is a mixture of what three religions?
5. What are some services religious groups provide for the people of Taiwan?

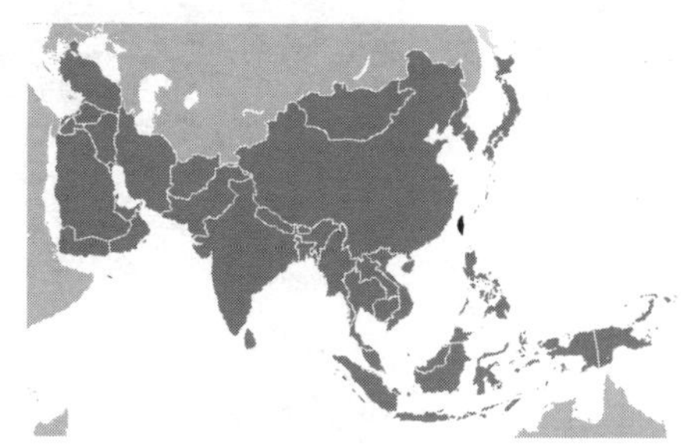

LESSON 9: Sports and Recreation

The six-day workweek has been popular in Taiwan for many years. Recently citizens have been seeking a more balanced lifestyle. They want to participate in sports and recreational activities. To allow citizens more time for these activities, the government started a new plan. It gives its employees, and most businesses, every other Saturday off. Workers now have more time to spend with their families and enjoy recreational activities. Citizens of Taiwan now earn enough money to spend more money than ever before on recreational activities. Golf has gained popularity and there are many golf courses on the island. In 1998 12 professional tournaments were held in Taiwan, and the prize money was nearly two million dollars. Sports that appeal to young people, such as surfing, scuba diving, and sailboarding are available and also very popular.

The Ministry of Education began the Sports for All People program in 1979 and built sports centers around the island. The centers include a track, swimming pool, gymnasium, and tennis courts. In addition, all school facilities are open to the public a few hours each day. Baseball is very popular, and there are thousands of Little League teams on the island.

Serious athletes can live and train at several centers in Taiwan. There is also a soccer stadium and two track and field arenas. There are professional basketball and baseball teams. Taiwan has competed in every Olympic Games and Asian Games since 1984, under the name *Chinese Taipei.*

This amusement park in Taiwan sits on a department store rooftop.

Group activities appeal to many Chinese people. Local corporations, government agencies, and schools have sports teams and clubs to give office workers some exercise. These activities include table tennis, basketball, softball, tennis, and badminton. Families enjoy amusement parks, and six national parks have been constructed.

You will find a mixture of old and new activities in the parks. People do folk dances, practice kung fu, play chess, do aerobics, or just jog and walk in the park, usually in the morning.

Nightlife in the cities of Taiwan is very active. Discos attract many young people. Karaoke television, called KTV, is popular. It is imported from Japan. A special microphone is used, with a collection of songs without lyrics. Singers choose the music and the video. As the words scroll out on a TV screen, they sing the song, and a special sound system mixes the voice with music. This creates a professional sound.

Within the cities, you will find traditional tea houses or tea art shops set in elegant gardens. They offer busy city people a place to escape the hustle and bustle of city life. Tea houses host art shows, antique shows, and displays of things such as teapots or dolls.

LESSON REVIEW

Directions: Number your paper from 1 to 4. Then answer the following questions.

1. How has the work week changed in recent years?
2. What is the name of the program started in 1979 by the Ministry of Education?
3. What facilities do sports centers include?
4. What is KTV?

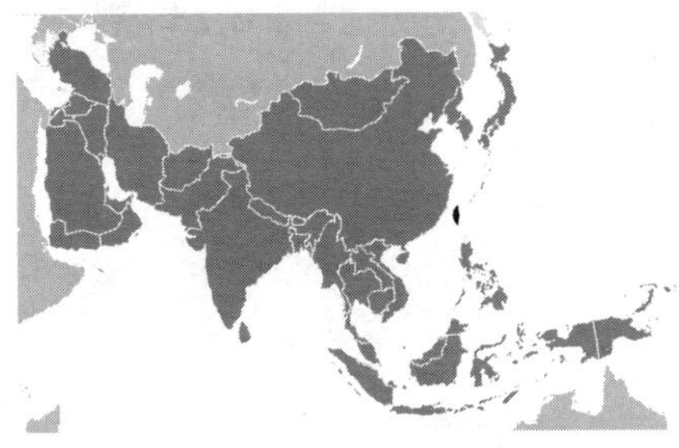

Spotlight Story

Improved Health Care

Taiwan has changed over the past 40 years from an agricultural country to a highly industrialized one. Along with this change have come new problems. As more people live longer, they have special health care needs. Serious air pollution and smoking problems have led to a high rate of lung cancer in many large cities. The increase of traffic in the cities has resulted in a high accident rate.

In 1985, the government realized that medical and health services needed to be improved and more evenly distributed throughout Taiwan. They divided the island into 17 medical care regions, each with hospitals, private doctors, and health stations. In 1997 more medical care was added to mountainous regions and the offshore islands. In 1998 medical care of the aging and the mentally ill was improved.

Great advances have been made in disease control. Forty years ago, serious diseases such as smallpox and cholera were the number-one killers. Today those diseases have been almost wiped out. There has been no malaria on Taiwan since 1965. Medicine keeps diseases such as tuberculosis, polio, and diphtheria under control. Cancer is the major cause of death among adults.

The government offers free checkups for cancer and AIDS, along with vaccinations for hepatitis. All school children receive immunizations. With the improvements in health care, people in Taiwan can now expect to live well into their 70s.

The Taiwanese government requires that all companies give their employees health insurance. The employees pay only a small part of the cost of this insurance. People over 70 and those with disabilities receive the insurance free. If a person is hospitalized, the insurance pays almost all the bills.

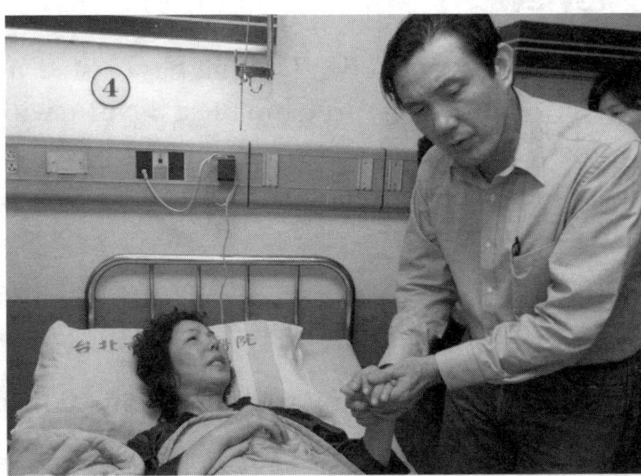

Traditional Chinese medicine has been used for thousands of years. In the past few years, it has received more respect from modern medical doctors and researchers in the United States and Canada. Acupuncture and other practices are studied to evaluate their effects on illnesses and diseases. The government funds these research projects.

SPOTLIGHT REVIEW

Answer the following questions.

1. What problems have resulted in Taiwan from its change from an agricultural to an industrial country?
2. What diseases that were once common are now almost wiped out?
3. How has the attitude of Western doctors changed toward traditional Chinese medicine?

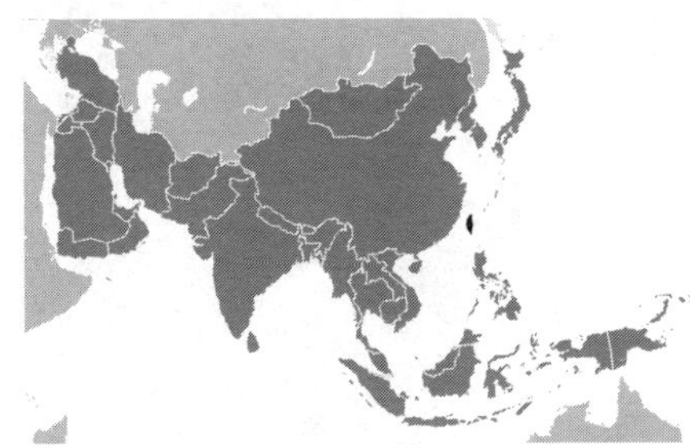

Chapter 4 Review

The country of Taiwan—Republic of China has existed since 1949. At that time, Nationalist forces in China lost a battle with Communist forces. The Nationalists escaped to Taiwan to set up their own government there. Relations between Taiwan and China have been tense since 1949.

Two-thirds of the island of Taiwan is covered with mountains that have forests on top.

Taiwan is one of the world's leading trading nations. The people of Taiwan place great importance on education, and Taiwanese have a high rate of literacy. The major religion in Taiwan is a mixture of Taoism, Confucianism, and Buddhism.

Over the years, Taiwan has changed from a poor nation to a wealthy, modern nation.

This Taiwan power plant is in mainland China.

Chapter 4 – Taiwan

Critical Thinking Skills

Directions: Think about the questions below. Then answer in complete sentences.

1. What are the differences between the governments in Taiwan and the People's Republic of China? How are citizens treated in each country?
2. If you lived in Taiwan, where would you live? Why?
3. How has health care changed in Taiwan over the past 40 years? Why has it changed?

For Discussion

1. Would your attitude toward school be different if you lived in Taiwan? Explain your answer.
2. How would your life be different if your parents had to work six days a week?

Write It!

Directions: Would you rather live in Taiwan or in China? Explain your answer.

For You to Do

Directions: Using the Internet or the library, look up some teachings of Confucius. Write a paragraph on his teachings.

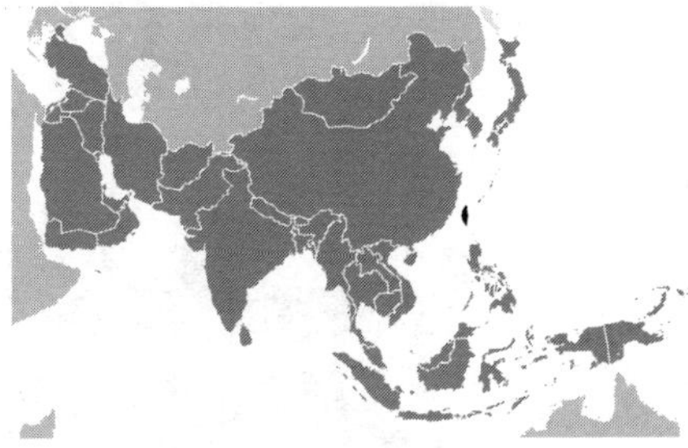

SOUTHEAST ASIA

CHAPTER 5

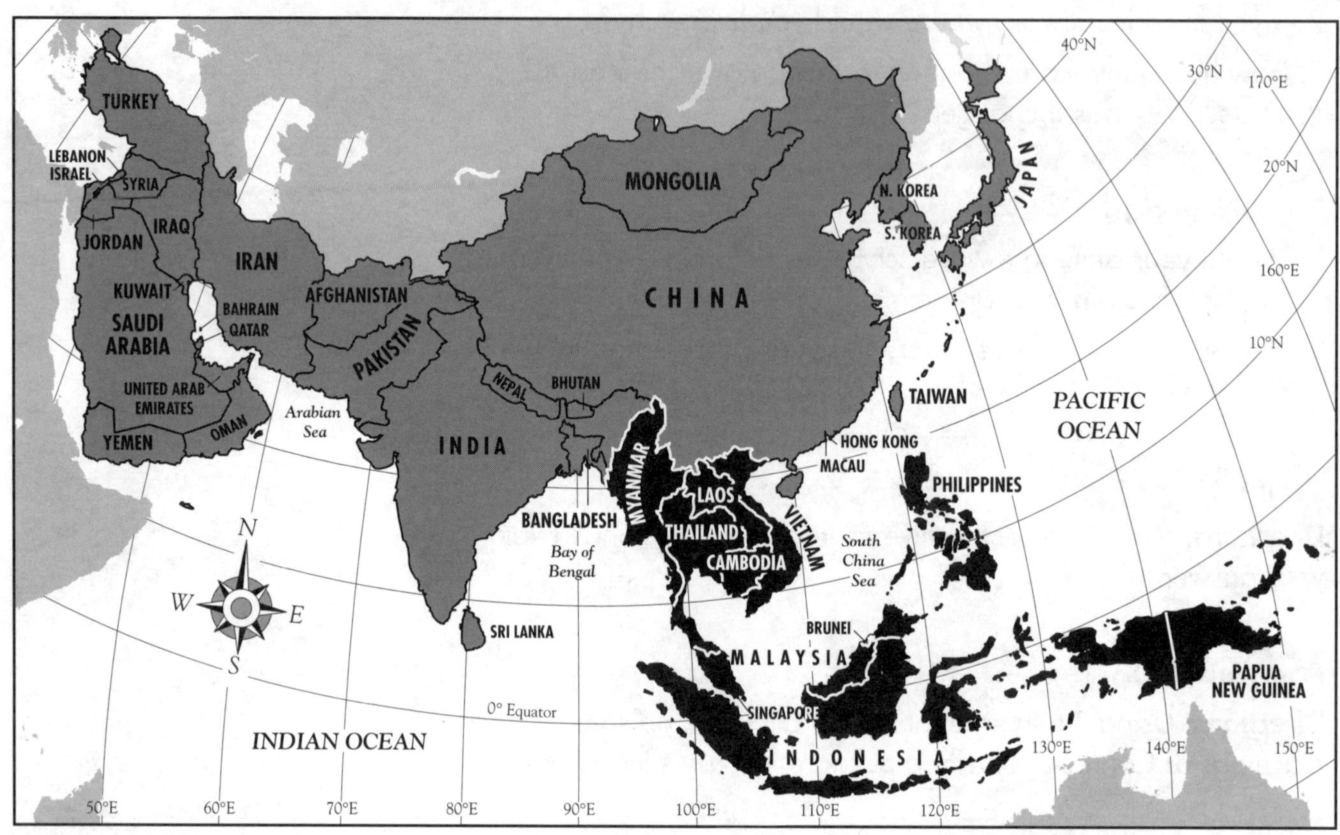

Fast Facts

- This area has thousands of islands that stretch across miles of water.
- Many languages, customs, and religions are found in Southeast Asia.
- The islands of Southeast Asia were once known as the Spice Islands.
- The farmers depend on the monsoon rains for growing their crops.

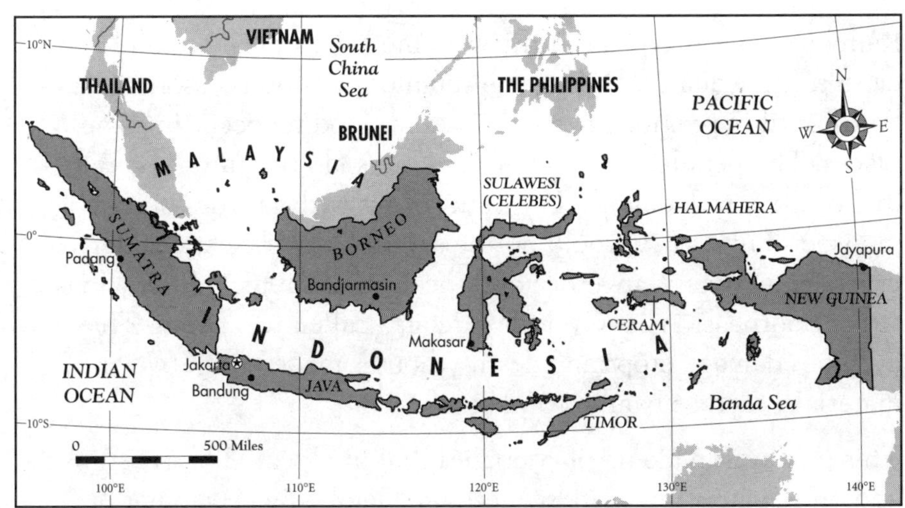

MAP SKILLS

Latitude and Longitude in Indonesia

Lines of latitude and longitude are imaginary lines drawn on a map. Latitude lines run east and west around the globe. Lines of longitude run north and south on a globe.

Directions: Study the map above to answer these questions.

1. What line of latitude is Timor near?
2. Padang is close to what line of latitude? What is this line called?
3. About how many miles is it from Jakarta to Bandung?
4. What body of water is southwest of Indonesia?
5. What city is near 140°E longitude?

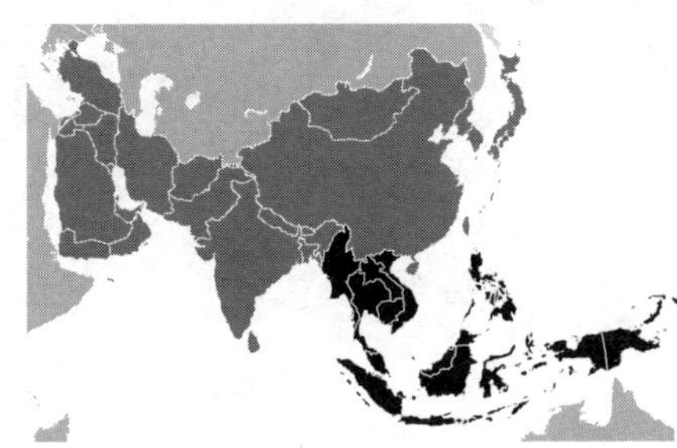

Words to Know

delta:
a deposit of soil, sand, and other materials at the mouth of a river

LESSON 1: A Variety of Land and Climates in Southeast Asia

Rainy weather is typical in this hot, muggy, tropical region located close to the equator. During the summer monsoon season, from April until September, heavy rains and flooding occur in some places. The people, especially the farmers, do not mind the rain—in fact, they welcome it! They know that without the summer monsoon rains, they would not be able to grow rice and other crops. Sometimes dangerous cyclones with extremely high winds strike Southeast Asia. Cyclones are also called tornadoes. These cyclones damage crops and destroy houses made of lightweight materials, such as bamboo and straw.

This region is made up of countries that are located on a peninsula and on neighboring islands. Vietnam, Cambodia, Myanmar or Burma, Laos and Thailand are on a section of land that juts into the South China Sea. The countries of Indonesia, Malaysia, Singapore, Brunei, and the Philippines are island nations.

The best farms in Southeast Asia are located in the **deltas** that are found near the mouths of rivers. Deltas are formed when rivers flood their banks and leave deposits of silt and other materials behind that make the soil rich. Lush, thick, green, tropical rain forests are found near the equator. The branches of very high trees form a canopy over all the other vegetation. Below the canopy is a wide variety of low-growing plants. Beautiful flowers, including orchids, grow in these moist forests. Thousands of insects, colorful tropical birds, and small animals can also be seen.

In the past, Southeast Asia was almost covered with forests. Today many trees have been cut down for lumber, burned for fuel, or cleared for farming. Some countries such as Cambodia, North Korea, South Korea, Indonesia, and Malaysia have lots of forestland left. But these forests are being destroyed very quickly. The wood is used to make beautiful, expensive furniture. A single teak log sells for as much as $200,000.

Some countries, such as Thailand, have preserved some of the forestland by creating parks for recreation. Thailand has placed a ban on logging since 1988 to preserve its forests. But the country still needs logs, so it imports them from other countries.

LESSON REVIEW

Directions: Number your paper from 1 to 5. Then answer the following questions.

1. Describe the climate and dangerous weather conditions of Southeast Asia.
2. How are deltas formed?
3. Why do the people of Southeast Asia welcome the summer monsoon season?
4. Describe a tropical rainforest.
5. Do you think many people live in tropical rain forests? Explain your answer.

THE VIETNAM WAR 1960-1975

After World War II, Vietnam was divided into North Vietnam, controlled by Communists, and South Vietnam, which was not Communist. The United States had been involved in this area of Southeast Asia in the 1950s. But when two U.S. ships were attacked off the coast of North Vietnam in 1964, U.S. involvement quickly increased.

Despite sending 500,000 American troops to fight in Vietnam, the United States could not win the war and began pulling out in 1969. After the United States had officially left Vietnam, the South Vietnamese government collapsed, and the North Vietnamese took control of Saigon, the capital of South Vietnam.

There was much disagreement among Americans about the war. It was often unclear who was winning the war, and many soldiers were killed. More than 20 years after the war ended, many Americans were still missing in action. In 1995, President Clinton announced that there would be full diplomatic relations with Vietnam.

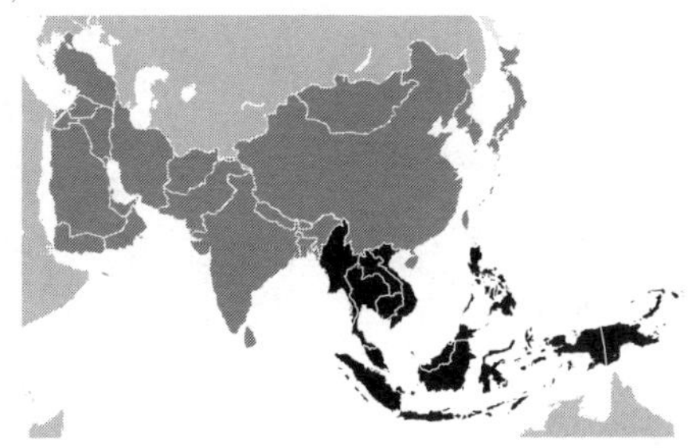

Words to Know

plantation:
a large farm that usually specializes in growing one crop, such as tobacco

LESSON 2: The People of the Peninsula

A small group of nomads still live on the peninsula in Southeast Asia. They hunt and fish for their food and often move from place to place. They are living much as their ancestors did. There are also several other ethnic groups whose language and customs keep them separated. In the following sections, you will take a closer look at the lands of the peninsula and the people who inhabit them.

Myanmar (Burma) and the Burmese

Myanmar, formerly called Burma, is the largest country on the peninsula. It has green fields and rolling hills. Most people live in the delta region of the Irrawaddy River.

Crops are easy to grow here because there is plenty of rainfall. Teak, a hard and very durable wood, grows in the forests of Myanmar. It is exported to countries around the world. Much of it is used in the United States to make fine, expensive furniture.

Most Burmese are devout Buddhists. Many religious statues and pagodas, or shrines devoted to religion, can be seen throughout the country.

Women in Myanmar never had to struggle for equal rights as women did in other countries. Burmese women have always been considered equal to men by law. Married women usually take care of the family finances. Women usually keep their maiden names when they marry.

Thailand and the Thais

Thailand is about three-quarters of the size of Texas. Forests and mountains are in the north. Tropical forests and beautiful beaches are found on the narrow Malay peninsula in the south.

During the rainy season, farmers produce large quantities of rice. Much of this rice is exported to other countries. Rubber is also grown on **plantations**. Teakwood, another natural product, comes from the forests.

Most of the Thais can read and write. They are followers of the Buddhist religion. They believe in tolerance, patience, and good nature towards others. Many refugees from other countries have moved to Thailand as a result of the wars in Vietnam and Cambodia.

Vietnam and the Vietnamese

The Vietnamese people have a mixed culture. They have borrowed traditions from the Chinese, French, and Indians. The Vietnamese are often shy and greet people with a slight bow, with the palms of their hands extended upward. They live very simply. The influence of Confucius and his teachings is seen among the rural people.

Laos and the Laotians

Laos is a land of jungles and mountains. The Mekong River runs along the western edge of the country and forms a fertile valley. Most of the people live in this valley. Laos is an underdeveloped country with very few industries or businesses. Most people in both the cities and rural areas are very poor.

The Laotians have a reputation for being peace-loving, modest, and friendly. They practice the Buddhist religion. Almost every man in Laos serves as a monk for some part of his life.

Cambodia and the Cambodians

The Mekong River flows through Laos and into Cambodia. In the past, the land provided people with the food they needed. This is not true today. Constant fighting and turmoil have caused many problems. People go hungry because not enough crops are being raised. Many have left their country to avoid starvation. Thousands of Cambodians are now living in Thailand and other countries.

About 90 percent of the population are descendents of the Khmers. The Khmers had one of the most powerful kingdoms in ancient times. The rest of the population are Vietnamese or Chinese who live in villages and are Buddhists.

LESSON REVIEW

Directions: Number your paper from 1 to 4. Then answer the following questions.

1. Which country of the peninsula has taken in refugees from other countries?
2. In which country of the peninsula are the people mostly Buddhists?
3. Why have people fled from Cambodia?
4. Which country of the peninsula do you think has the best living conditions? Why?

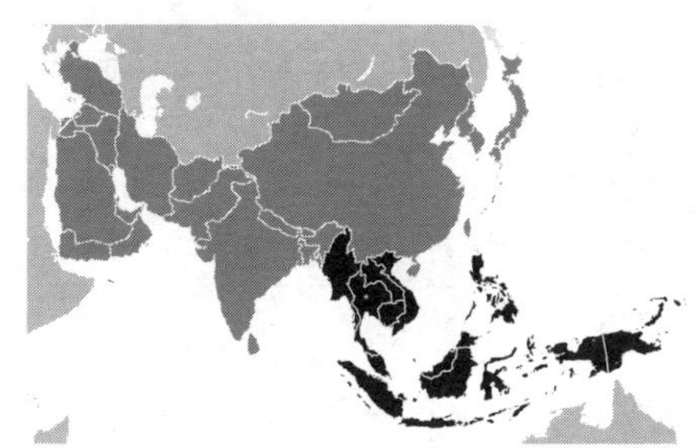

Words to Know

barren:
does not produce; has small amount or no vegetation

descent:
family line, ancestors

diverse:
different from something else; varied

LESSON 3: The People of the Islands

It is hard to imagine that there are over 20,000 islands and smaller islets that make up the island nations of Southeast Asia. Hardly any two of these islands are alike. Many are not inhabited because they are **barren**, rocky, swampy, or volcanic. Other islands, such as Java in Indonesia, are overpopulated because of the fertile farmland found there.

Malaysia and the Malaysians

Malaysia stretches from the tip of Thailand to the Philippine Islands. The country has three different states: Malaya, Sarawak, and Sabah. Sarawak and Sabah are on the island of Borneo. Brunei, a small independent country since 1984, is also on the island with the Malaysian states. Brunei is a very wealthy nation because of oil deposits. The rest of the island of Borneo is part of Indonesia.

The rubber plantations and tin deposits found in Malaysia have made it one of the richest Asian nations. The people of Malaysia are **diverse**. The largest group is the Malay Muslims. In the cities, many Chinese people can be found. The Pakistanis and the Indians are another large group.

This woman is gathering medicinal herbs in a Malaysian rainforest.

Singapore and the Singaporeans

Singapore is a tiny island near the Malaysian peninsula. It is one of the wealthiest countries in Southeast Asia.

Most of the people live in the city of Singapore. This city is built around a harbor and has tall buildings, department stores, apartment buildings, and many shops.

About 70 percent of the population of Singapore is Chinese. Most of the people are in some type of business. Loading and unloading ships in the busy harbor provides work for many people.

Indonesia and the Indonesians

Approximately 13,700 Indonesian islands and smaller islets sprawl over a distance of about 3,200 miles.Three of the islands are Sumatra, Java, and Sulawesi.

The main island of Java is one of the most densely populated places in the world. More than 108 million people live on this small island. Jakarta, its capital, is the largest city in Southeast Asia.

Philippine Islands and the Filipinos

Of the 7,000 Philippine islands, only about one-third are inhabited. Many islands have rich soil and many natural resources. The tropical climate is good for farming and lumbering.

Most Filipinos are a mixture of Malaysian, Spanish, Chinese, Indian, and Arabian **descent**. Many are peasants who work for wealthy farmers that own most of the land.

Christianity is the main religion of the Philippines. They adopted the Roman Catholic religion from the Spanish who controlled the islands from 1500 to 1898.

LESSON REVIEW

Directions: Number your paper from 1 to 4. Then answer the following questions.

1. What types of land are found on the islands of Southeast Asia?
2. Why is Malaysia one of the richest Southeast Asia countries?
3. Which island of Indonesia is the most densely populated? Why?
4. Why do you think that the Philippines is the only Southeast Asian country where the majority of people are Christian?

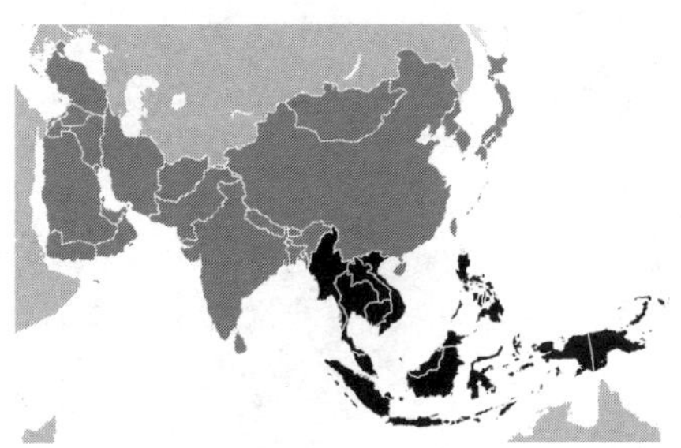

Words to Know

dominate:
rule or control

exile:
to remove or banish; separate from one's home or country

LESSON 4: Southeast Asia: Yesterday and Today

The first kingdoms in Southeast Asia were built by people who migrated from China. They were skilled in shipbuilding and trading. The Khmer Empire **dominated** most of this area from 800 to 1200.

Spices Bring the Europeans

Most spices we use today—such as pepper, cinnamon, and cloves—grow in the tropical climate of this region. During the 1500s, Europeans discovered these spices. They took the spices back to Europe where they became very popular. Soon the Europeans were willing to pay high prices for them, and Southeast Asia became known as the Spice Islands.

Many European nations tried to control the spice trade because these spices brought such high prices. The Dutch finally managed to gain control of the spices of Indonesia, where they began a plantation system. These plantations still exist today.

Southeast Asia Today

Most Southeast Asian countries are now independent, but unrest continues. Myanmar (Burma), Vietnam, Laos, and Cambodia are recovering from European arrivals in Southeast Asia.

European Arrivals in Southeast Asia

1511	Portuguese seized city of Malacca on Malay peninsula
1521	Magellan claimed Philippines for Spain
1571	Spain gained complete control of Philippines
1615	French sent missionaries to Vietnam
1641	Dutch won control of area around Jakarta, Indonesia
1819	British came to Singapore
1859	French invaded Vietnam
1886	British gained control of Burma
1941	Japanese overran many countries in Southeast Asia; the countries rebelled and lost their independence in the destruction of war.

Struggle Towards Democracy

Several countries are struggling to gain or maintain a democratic government. Malaysia is a good example of a struggling government. Malaysia's many different cultural groups makes governing difficult. The Malays have always distrusted the Chinese, who run most of the businesses.

The Philippine islands have a constitution and elected officials, but the government does not always run smoothly. In 1972 President Marcos's term as president ended, but he refused to give up the office. Instead he seized military control of the government. He shut down all communications on the island and jailed his opponents. In the next election, he was defeated by Corizon Aquino. Her husband, an opponent of Marcos, had been murdered a few years before. The battle between Aquino and Marcos continued even after Marcos's death. Marcos died while in **exile** from his native country. Aquino did not wish him to be buried in the Philippines.

Indonesia's government has been somewhat stable. President Suharto was in office from 1968 to 1998. When he took the job as president, the Communist Party was threatening to take over the government. Today, however, communism is banned in Indonesia, and Indonesia is a republic. Abdurrahman Wahid became president in 1999.

The economy has improved steadily, but it cannot keep up with the population growth. The government has started a relocation program. Families are offered land, a two-room house, and farm equipment if they will move to another less populated island.

LESSON REVIEW

Directions: Number your paper from 1 to 4. Then answer the following questions.

1. Where did the first people of Southeast Asia come from?
2. Why did the Europeans want control of the countries in Southeast Asia?
3. Which countries of Southeast Asia have a form of democratic government?
4. Describe the events leading to the election of Corizon Aquino.

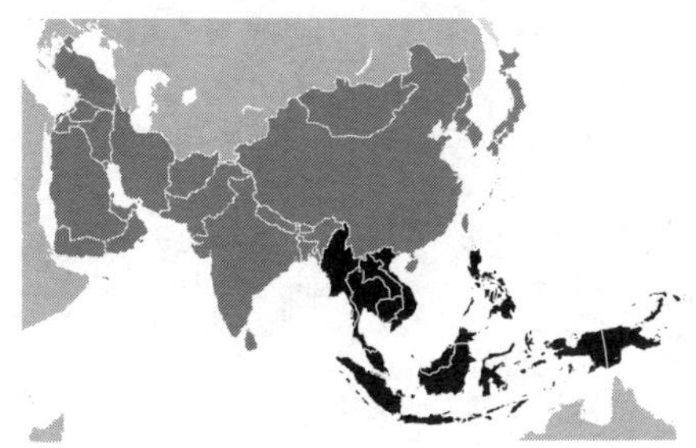

Words to Know

rickshaws:
a form of transportation in which a small two-wheeled carriage is pulled by a man

slash and burn:
cutting down and burning trees to clear land, usually for farming

subsistence:
the production of just enough food to feed a farmer's family

LESSON 5: Life in Southeast Asia

Most people of Southeast Asia live in the countryside in small villages or farms. The communities are found along the rivers or near the coast. The people who live in these villages are **subsistence** farmers.

The river valleys of Myanmar (Burma), Thailand, and Vietnam have the best rice fields in Southeast Asia. In this part of the region it is common to see men, women, and children standing knee-deep in water and tending the rice.

This woman is tending a rice field.

Some countries do not let farmers own their own land. In Vietnam, for example, farm communes are state-owned. Members of the commune are paid for their work. In other countries, however, private ownership of land is common. On the island of Java, for example, eight out of every ten farmers are landowners, even though they own a very small amount of the land.

In the Philippines, farming methods have not changed much over the years. Water buffalo still pull the plows, and crops are still harvested by hand in some places. The villages in the Philippines are called barangays. The people build their houses on stilts because of flooding during the heavy rains. Some of the Filipino farmers are very poor. They do not own their farmland. It is owned by wealthy landowners who pay the peasant farmers to work the land.

Plantations in some of the countries produce crops for the world market. Malaysia has rubber plantations, and more than one-third of the world's supply comes from this nation. Indonesia, in addition to rubber plantations, has coffee, tea, sugar, and tobacco plantations. Many plantations in Southeast Asia are owned by Americans and Europeans.

People in the Philippines build their houses on stilts so they don't get flooded during heavy rains.

Forests Are Important in Southeast Asia

Indonesia has the most forests in the region with more than 300 million acres of hardwood trees. This hardwood is in demand worldwide. Myanmar (Burma) supplies 80 percent of the world's teakwood. In the Philippines, forests are also plentiful. They cover about half of the land. The kapok tree grows in the Philippines. This tree produces a fiber, also called kapok, that is used in insulation, mattresses, and upholstery.

Poor logging methods are causing the forests of Indonesia and other areas to disappear. Flooding occurs when forests are removed too fast. The **slash and burn** method farmers use in hilly areas causes this problem. The farmers cut down and burn the trees to clear the land for their crops. Soon, they move on to another area and repeat the process. All the countries of Southeast Asia are beginning programs to stop this practice in order to save their valuable forests.

City Life

Although most of the population of Southeast Asia live in rural areas, a few large cities exist. Every country has one major city, usually the capital. Examples include Yangon (Rangoon), Myanmar (Burma); Jakarta, Indonesia; and Bangkok, Thailand.

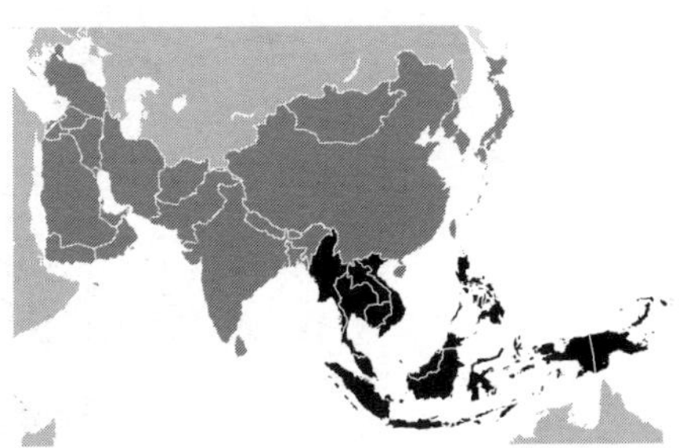

The people on the left are selling spring onions from their bicycle baskets.

The large cities of Southeast Asia have some modern sections that include office buildings and factories. In the port cities, large ships deliver manufactured products and pick up raw goods such as rubber, oil, and timber. The streets of most of these cities are very crowded. Cars, trucks, buses, trolley cars, bicycles, **rickshaws**, oxcarts, and people fill the streets. In the older sections are markets that sell a variety of fresh fish, vegetables, and even live chickens!

These are some of the large cities of Southeast Asia:

Jakarta, Indonesia—This city on the island of Java is a mixture of green trees, canals, shanty towns, huts, and mansions. A ten-lane boulevard runs through the center of Jakarta. Along this boulevard are foreign embassies, modern hotels, and high-rise office buildings. On the outskirts of Jakarta are the *kampongs*, or villages of the peasants.

Bangkok, Thailand—Bangkok has many *klongs*, or canals, that have very important functions. Sampans, a type of boat, deliver fruits and vegetables to the markets along the canals. Rice and lumber also come into the city by way of the canals. Hundreds of houseboats are tied to the side of these canals. Entire families live on these houseboats. The houseboats are not very long; they are about the length of two rowboats. Houseboat residents cook on charcoal fires and sleep on mats that are stowed away during the day. Clothes are washed in the canal and spread on the roof to dry. Bangkok has a modern section with streets jammed with cars, trucks, buses, and motorcycles. Department stores, office buildings, railroad stations, and an airport can be found in this section of the city.

Manila, Philippines—Manila has modern office buildings, shops, apartments, and a rapid transit system. *Jeepneys*, or taxis, are a common sight in Manila. These taxis are shared by as many people as can fit! The jeepneys are built from old jeeps that the U.S. Army left behind after World War II.

Sampans deliver fruits and vegetables to the markets along the canals in Bangkok.

Kuala Lumpur, Malaysia—This city is spread out on both sides of the Klong River and is extremely crowded. Rubber and tin processing are the main industries in and near the city. The people of Kuala Lumpur are a mixture of Indian, Chinese, Malaysian, and European. One entire section of the city is Chinese. Most of these people are merchants.

Many of the Indians in Kuala Lumpur came to the city as merchants or laborers to work on the large rubber plantations. These Indians cling to the language and customs of their homeland. They have also taken on some of the customs of Europeans who came to Malaysia. For example, some of the Indians are Roman Catholic, and the children speak English as taught in the Catholic schools.

LESSON REVIEW

Directions: Number your paper from 1 to 4. Then answer the following questions.

1. Where do most Southeast Asians live?
2. What are some types of crops that are grown on plantations?
3. Why are the forests of Indonesia disappearing?
4. Why do you think people continue to flock to the cities where they may have to live in poverty?

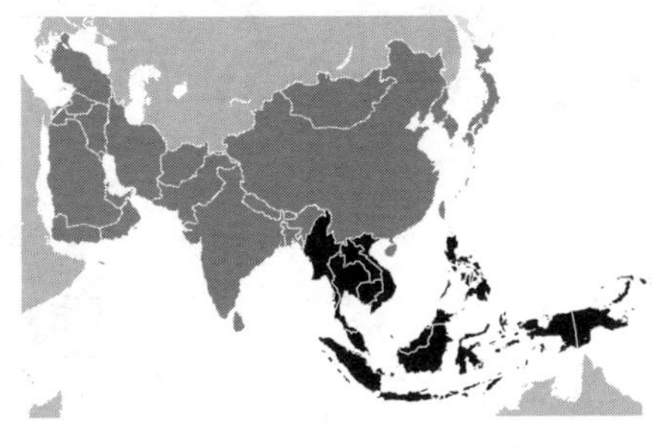

LESSON 6: Religions and Education

Southeast Asia has a greater variety of religions than any other region of the world. Most of the religions were begun in other countries and then brought to the area. Buddhism and Hinduism came from India; Islam from the Middle East; Confucianism and Taoism from China, and Christianity from the West. The people respect one another's religions. Some are followers of parts of two faiths. A person may be a Muslim but also follow some Buddhist traditions and practice its rituals. On the mainland of Southeast Asia in the countries of Thailand, Laos, Vietnam, and Cambodia, most people are Buddhists. The island countries have a majority of Muslims who practice the Islam religion. More Muslims live in Indonesia than in any other nation, including the Arab countries of the Middle East. The Islamic religion began in the Middle East with the teachings of Muhammad. Muhammad was born in Arabia. His teachings are written in the sacred book, the Koran.

The Muslims of Southeast Asia follow the basic beliefs of Islam but have adapted some of them to fit their lifestyle. For example, men usually have only one wife.

Confucianisms

Have you ever heard of Confucius or any of his sayings? Confucius was a teacher and philosopher who was born in China in 551 B.C. His teachings and philosophies were adopted by many countries in Southeast Asia. Confucius wanted people to lead good, moral lives and to be loyal and hardworking. Most of his teachings and philosophies were written down. The wise sayings of Confucius are often quoted. Listed below are some of them.

On making mistakes: "Our greatest glory is not in falling, but in rising every time we fall."

On ignorance: "Ignorance is the night of the mind, but a night without a moon or stars."

On education: "Study the past if you would divine (predict) the future."

On avoiding wickedness: "To see and listen to the wicked is already the beginning for wickedness."

On treatment of others: "What you do not want done to yourself, do not do to others."

This practice is different from what Muhammad taught. Muhammad said that men could have many wives. Another adaptation of the Islamic religion concerns praying. The Koran says a Muslim should pray five times a day and also pray on Fridays at a mosque. Most Indonesians pray only on Fridays. They do not stop what they are doing and pray five times each day as other Muslims do. In Java, however, the rule concerning praying is strictly followed. Most Muslims in Java kneel, facing Mecca, and pray five times a day.

Buddhism

Buddhism is the main religion of the countries on Southeast Asia's peninsula. Its influence on the culture can be seen by the large numbers of Buddhist statues, shrines, and pagodas throughout the countries. In the cities the yellow-robed monks walk the streets among the common people. Each year many young men, some only eleven or twelve years old, leave their homes to go to the monasteries to study to become monks. Some stay only a few months, some a few years, and others stay their whole lives. Monks are highly respected by all Buddhists and are considered the closest people to Buddha. Many monks become teachers, and all are honored during religious ceremonies and festivals.

Christianity

Catholic missionaries came to Southeast Asia in the sixteenth century. The French missionaries brought Christianity to Vietnam. Spain, a predominantly Catholic country, sent missionaries to the Philippines to teach their religion. Today, the Philippines remains the only country in Southeast Asia whose population is made up mostly of Christians. About 95 percent of the population is Christian, and 85 percent of those people are Roman Catholics.

The Filipinos have added some special things to their religious customs. In the Roman Catholic communities, processions and ceremonies are held to honor special saints. Each village chooses a saint as its protector and honors the saint on special days. There is usually a parade with music, flowers, food, games, and sometimes fireworks.

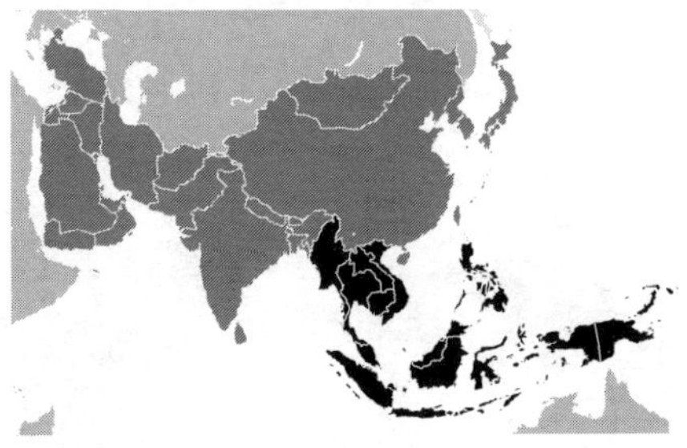

Words to Know

caste:
a system of social classes dividing Hindus

illiterate:
not able to read or write; uneducated

reincarnation:
a belief in the rebirth of the soul of a person into a new body or different form

Hinduism

Hinduism is the main religion of India and was brought to Southeast Asia by the Indians. Hindus worship many gods and believe in **reincarnation**. They also believe in the **caste** system that divides people into social classes. Hindus believe that people are born into a caste and must do the same kind of work as the other members. Hinduism never became popular in Southeast Asia, except on the island of Bali in Indonesia.

These dancers are honoring a Hindu god.

Taoism

Taoism is a religion that began in China. *Tao* means "way." Taoists believe people should be satisfied with their lives and should not try to change them. The Taoist ideal is a simple, meditative life that is close to nature. Ceremonies and rituals are not important to the Taoists. Taoism is practiced in Vietnam more than any other country.

Confucianism

Confucianism is not really a religion but an ancient philosophy. It is based on the teachings of a wise Chinese man named Confucius. He believed that people should trust one another, obey their rulers, and respect their elders. He also said that people should lead a good, moral life. Confucianism is widespread in Asian countries.

Education in Southeast Asia

In the past, children were educated in religious schools. These were the only schools in most countries. The Buddhist and Muslim schools taught reading and writing. In Vietnam, the schools taught the writings of Confucius. Even though these schools existed, many village people did not attend. They concentrated on learning the skills needed for survival, such as farming, woodworking, and metalworking. Many village people were **illiterate**.

Today, the governments of most countries have opened schools in cities and in rural areas. Most countries require students to attend school for at least three years. Although a large number of children start school, many drop out because of poor health and poverty or because they may live a long distance from the school. One exception is Myanmar (Burma), where children ages five through nine must attend school.

LESSON REVIEW

Directions: Number your paper from 1 to 5. Then answer the following questions.

1. In which countries are most people Buddhists? In which countries are the people mostly Muslim?
2. What part do monks have in the Buddhist religion? Why do you think so many young boys become monks?
3. How have the Muslims of Southeast Asia changed or adapted the ceremonies of Islam to fit their lifestyle?
4. Why do you think Confucianism is not considered a religion but a philosophy?
5. Why do you think Christianity has not taken hold in most Southeast Asian countries?

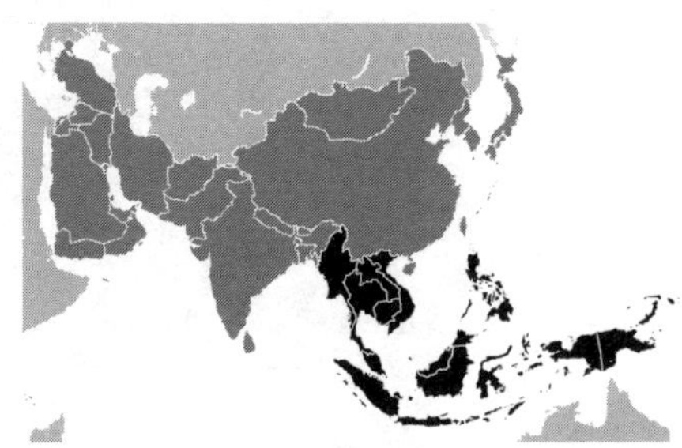

LESSON 7: The Arts and Entertainment

Many long stories, or epics, written in India and China are also enjoyed in Southeast Asian countries. These stories have been translated and performed as plays. The writings of Confucius are the most popular form of literature. Even people who can't read memorize and recite the wise sayings of Confucius, just as many Christian people recite passages from the Bible.

Music and Dancing

Almost every village in Southeast Asia has a *gamelin*, or small orchestra. Several percussion instruments give the music a loud, distinctive beat. Flutes and cellos carry the melody in a high pitched sound.

Accompanied by the gamelin, folk dancers perform during festivals. These dancers wear brightly colored costumes and tell stories by using graceful hand and body movements. These movements are difficult to learn. Girls begin learning the dances when they are very young. Only the best dancers are chosen to perform during religious festivals and ceremonies.

The Elephant Round-up takes place every November in the town of Surin, Thailand.

Festivals Are a Part of Religion

Have you ever gone to a show or play that has lasted all night? During an important Hindu religious festival, the Burmese enjoy a very long show called a *pwe*, and it sometimes lasts all night! The pwe is a mixture of theatre, comedy, music, and dancing. The show is held outside, and people come with their mats to sit on the ground and watch. Some even bring food to enjoy and share with their friends. They are entertained by wizards, magicians, talking animals, and story tellers.

Shadow plays are popular in Indonesian villages. Puppets are moved between a lamp and a screen to cast shadows. The puppet master tells the story. People in the cities go to movies, watch TV, and enjoy Western rock music.

During the Buddhist New Year in Myanmar (Burma) and other Buddhist countries, the people have a Water Festival. This celebration can last for three days. People throw water at one another in a spirit of joy. They may use buckets, water balloons, and even fire hoses. The water supposedly washes away past bad deeds. There are shouts of "Happy New Year" as the water is thrown.

Sports

Sports in Southeast Asia are especially popular in and near the cities. Football, basketball, swimming, and boxing are some of the favorites. The Thais and Burmese enjoy kick-boxing. The matches are fierce and fast-moving. People in Indonesia practice *penchak*, a different kind of boxing, more like self-defense. It is often accompanied by music and sometimes it looks like dancing rather than boxing.

Games

Southeast Asians enjoy games that use grace and skill. *Chinlon* is a popular game played with a 4-inch ball made of bamboo strips. Players stand in a circle. They use their feet to try to kick a ball and keep it in the air. The game is more of an exhibition than a contest, because players try to help each other keep the ball aloft.

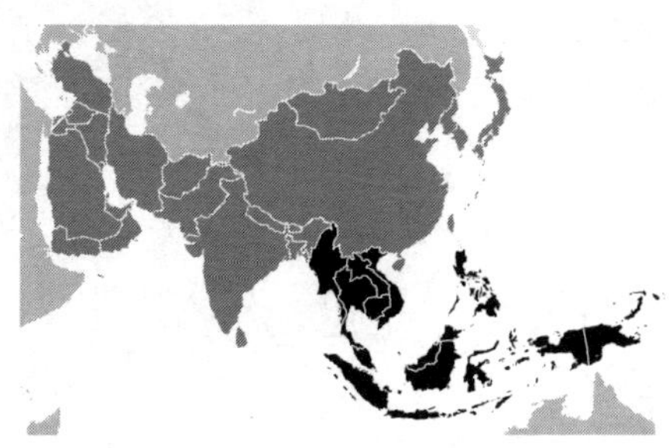

Kite-flying has always been popular with young and old. In Bangkok, contests take place during the spring. This activity is especially popular when the strong monsoon winds blow. Other pastimes include bull races in Thailand and cockfights in Malaysia, Indonesia, and in the Philippines. In Singapore, a Chinese game called mah-jongg is popular. It is a complicated card game played with tiles, somewhat like dominoes.

Kite-flying contests are held every spring in Bangkok, Thailand.

LESSON REVIEW

Directions: Number your paper from 1 to 5. Then answer the following questions.

1. What is a small village orchestra called? Describe the music it plays.
2. What is a pwe? Describe what you would see if you went to a pwe.
3. When and where is the Water Festival held? What does the throwing of water mean to a Burmese?
4. Why do you think sports are more popular in the cities than in the country?
5. Compare the popular sports of Southeast Asia to the popular sports of the United States. Why do you think popular sports in the United States, such as football and baseball, are not as popular in Southeast Asia?

Spotlight Story

Life of a Buddhist Monk

Southeast Asia has a large number of Buddhists. Many boys at the age of 12, or even younger, enter a Buddhist monastery to study to become monks. This is usually the most important day of their lives. The villages where the boys live hold celebrations to honor each boy who becomes a monk. After the celebration, the boy's head is shaved and he is given a Buddhist name. From then on he wears a simple yellow robe. His only possessions are a begging bowl, a sleeping mat, and an umbrella to shade him from the hot tropical sun.

Life is harsh for a boy at the monastery. The monks rise early in the morning to pray together. Then they walk to nearby communities and beg for rice and money. The rest of the day is spent at the monastery performing rituals, such as chanting and praying. They also study holy books and spend time alone to meditate.

Monks can leave the monastery at any time. They do not have to stay for their whole lives. Many young boys find that the life is too harsh and lonely and return to their villages. The ones that stay follow a regular course of study so that they may teach others.

Each village has a monastery and the people of the village invite monks to live there. The monk has two important roles in the village: to teach the children and to take part in Buddhist rituals when invited. The people want the monks to come to their villages. They feel they earn blessings by taking care of the monks.

SPOTLIGHT REVIEW

Answer the following questions.

1. Name two things a young boy must do when entering a Buddhist monastery.
2. What do the monks do during their day, once they are living in the monastery?
3. Do all monks remain at the monastery for life? Explain your answer.
4. When a monk goes to a village to live, what are his main duties?

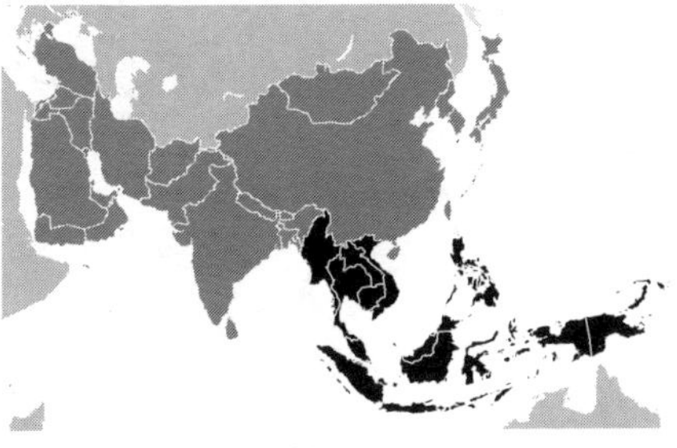

Chapter 5 Review

Southeast Asia is made up of countries on the peninsula south of China and many island nations. The climate is hot, humid, and rainy.

Southeast Asia has a greater variety of religions than any other region in the world. Buddhism is practiced in many countries. However, the island nations are mostly Muslims, except for the Philippines, which has a majority of Christians. Hinduism is the main religion of India. Taoism is practiced in Vietnam more than in any other country. Confucianism is widespread.

Poor logging methods are causing forests in many Southeast Asian nations to disappear. Most of the people live in rural areas. Education is improving, and literacy rates are rising in many countries. The arts, including architecture and literature, are usually associated with religion. Sports are very popular, especially in the cities. Most Southeast Asian countries are independent, but unrest continues.

This woman is a member of the Akha ethnic group in Thailand.

Critical Thinking Skills

Directions: Give some thought to the questions below. Be sure to answer in complete sentences.

1. What are three ways the people living in the island countries of Southeast Asia earn a living?
2. Which religions of Southeast Asia do you think seem to have the greatest affect on the daily lives of the people? Give examples to support your answer.
3. If you visited Southeast Asia, what city would you like to see? Why?
4. How do you think the Southeast Asian governments can improve education for the children?
5. On a trip to Southeast Asia, what type of entertainment or activities would you see people enjoying? Which would you like to see?

For Discussion

1. Why do you think slash and burn farming is so widely used? What other methods might be tried?
2. What advice do you think Confucius might give to modern people to help them live good lives? Write a Confucianism of your own.
3. Why do you think there are so many different religious beliefs in most of Southeast Asia?
4. Which industries or crop productions might be improved in order to help the Southeast Asian countries develop economically?
5. Do you think the struggling democratic countries of Malaysia, Indonesia, and the Philippines will remain democratic? Do you think the United States should help these governments? Why or why not?

Write It!

Directions: Plan a trip to Southeast Asia. Tell how you would get there, the kind of clothing you would bring, and what you would like to see. Use library materials or contact a travel agent for additional information.

For You to Do

Directions: Research additional material on refugees that come into the United States from Southeast Asia. Write a report describing any procedures these people have to go through in order to come into this country legally. How do you think it would feel to be a refugee? Why do you think these people would want to leave their country for a new life in the United States?

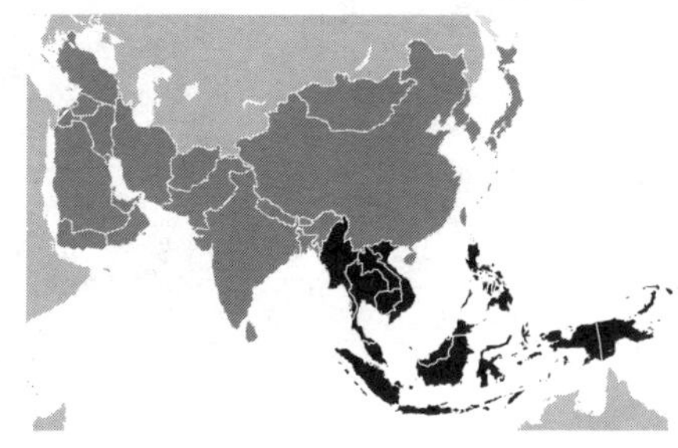

INDIA

CHAPTER 6

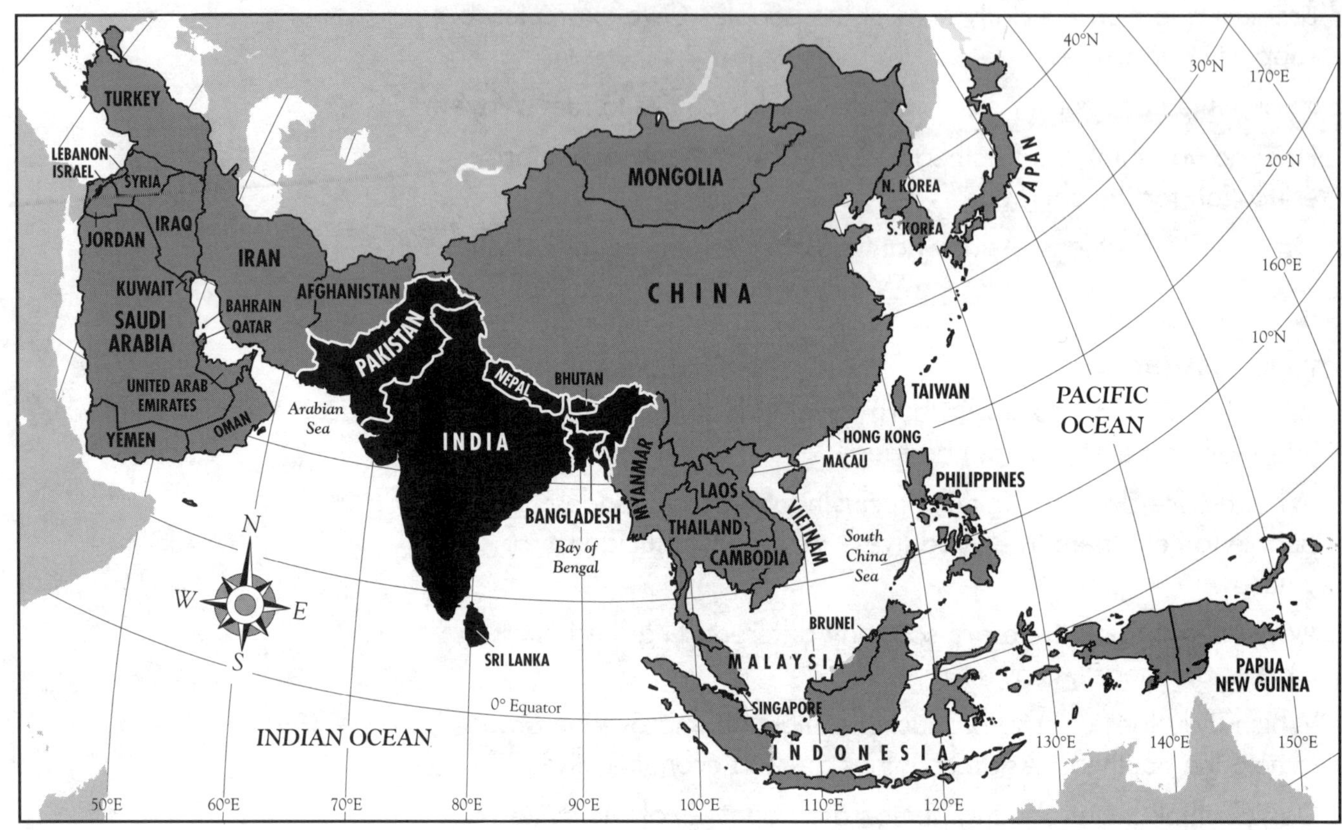

Fast Facts

- India is the largest country in Southern Asia.
- India is one of the top five countries in the production of computer software.
- India is densely populated—only China has more people.
- Many ancient civilizations began in the Indus River valley.

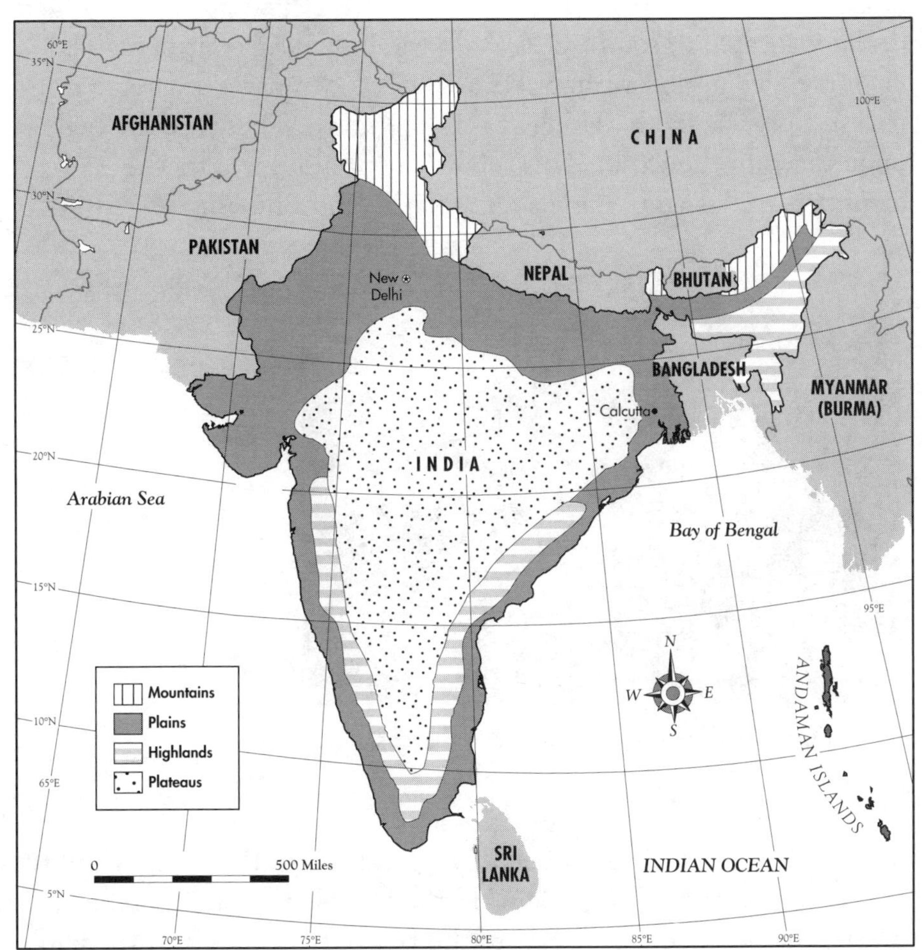

MAP SKILLS

Relief Map of India

A relief map shows the kinds of land found in a country. India is made up of mountains, plains, highlands, and plateaus.

Directions: Study the map above to answer these questions.

1. New Delhi and Calcutta are located on the same type of land. What kind of land is this?
2. What type of land makes up the central part of India?
3. Which neighboring countries have no mountains on their borders?
4. What type of land is found between the plateaus and the plains?
5. What type of land is most often seen east of Bangladesh?

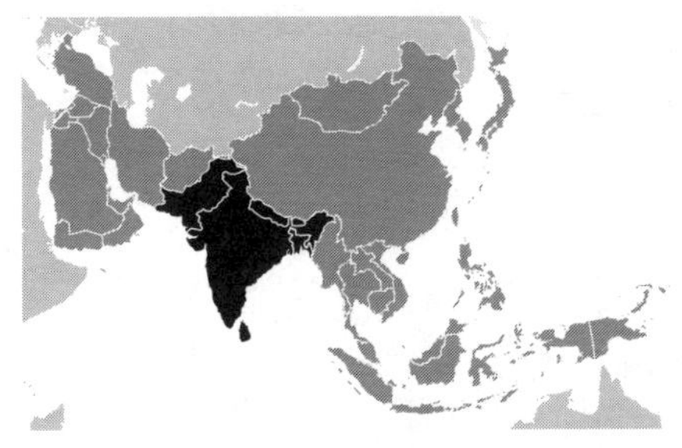

Chapter 6 – India

LESSON 1: India Is the Largest Country in Southern Asia

India is located in southern Asia on the Indian subcontinent. This area is called a subcontinent because it is a peninsula separated from the rest of Asia by the Himalayas to the north. These are the highest mountains in the world. This subcontinent also includes the countries of Pakistan, Bangladesh, Nepal, and Bhutan.

The Himalayas separate India from the rest of Asia.

In the northern part of India are two great rivers, the Ganges and the Indus. The Ganges River begins in the Himalayas and flows down into India. It travels southeast to the Bay of Bengal. Along the banks of this river is a broad, fertile plain. The Indus River in the northwest also flows down from the Himalayas. Along this river, both in India and Pakistan, is the Punjab region. The soil is rich in both the Ganges Valley and Punjab region because mud and silt are left on the land when the rivers flood. The mud and silt make the soil fertile and good for farming. Half of the people of India live and farm in these areas.

Chapter 6 – India

One of the most densely populated places in the world is the delta region of the Ganges and Brahmaputra Rivers. This delta, made up of rich soil washed down by the two rivers, is formed near the Bay of Bengal. It is an important farming region in India. In the United States there is a similar delta where the Mississippi River flows into the Gulf of Mexico. It has always been an important farming area. Many of these delta regions, in India and elsewhere, were among the first places people settled and built their cities. In India the great city of Calcutta began in the delta near the Bay of Bengal.

The southern part of India is a peninsula. A plateau is in the center of this peninsula. The coastal plains that extend to the oceans are on both sides of the plateau. They are separated from the plateau by mountains known as the Eastern and Western Ghats. These coastal plains are fertile and heavily populated. Farming is very good on these coastal plains. A large desert area in India extends from Pakistan into southwestern India. Few people live in this desert.

Climate Influenced by the Monsoon Winds

The climate of India is hot and humid in the areas where most people live. The mountain and highland areas have cooler weather. Much of India's climate is affected by the monsoon winds. The monsoon winds blow across much of India in both summer and winter. They cause the climate to be very dry in winter and very wet in summer.

The monsoon winds blow from the south from June until September, and they bring heavy rains. The farmers and people look forward to the monsoon season because it brings the moisture needed for farming. The land becomes swampy and muddy. The rivers overflow their banks, but in some areas dams control the flooding. The people know that when the rain stops, the dry season will come. The land will then become parched and dry because the monsoon winds blow from the north and bring dry air.

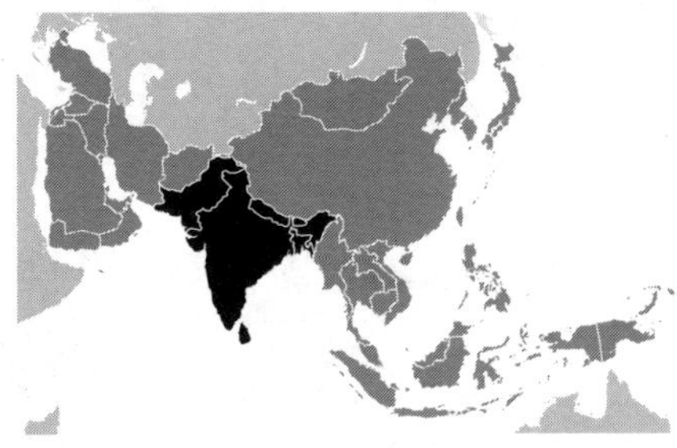

Words to Know

forebear:
ancestor

Even though India has large rivers and is surrounded by water on the southern peninsula, it is dry for much of the year. Without the monsoon winds to bring the heavy rains, little farming could be done.

LESSON REVIEW

Directions: Number your paper from 1 to 5. Then answer the following questions.

1. What two great rivers are in northern India? Why are they important?
2. What is a delta?
3. What happens during the summer monsoons? Why do the people and farmers look forward to the summer monsoons?
4. Do you think many people live on the plateau in the center of the peninsula? Explain your answer.
5. Do you think the average Indian knows much about the people of the neighboring Asian countries? Why or why not?

LESSON 2: The Early History of India

It is likely that people came to the rich valleys of the Indus River about 200,000 years ago. The early inhabitants grew food and made tools and pottery. Big cities as well as farming communities developed. These civilizations were so advanced that they had many of the modern comforts we have today, such as running water. They also traded with other cities in that part of the world.

Changes began to take place when invaders, the Aryans, came down from the plains in the north and settled all over India. The Aryans drove the Dravidians into the south, where many still live today. The Aryans brought with them such things as metal tools and a language called Sanskrit. The religion they brought with them was known as Brahmanism, which includes a belief in reincarnation. Out of this earlier belief grew the beginnings of the Hindu religion. Hinduism has remained the major religion of India.

The Aryans lived in religious or military groups ruled by Rajahs. The Aryan people thought they were better than the Indian people they had conquered. The Aryans would have nothing to do with the Indians. This attitude led to the formation of several different classes among the people. These classes did not associate with one another and did different types of work. Eventually, this division led to the Indian caste system still followed, although it is less strict than it once was. Many people in India, especially in the villages, still work and live their whole lives as members of the caste into which they were born.

Other People Also Invaded India

Many rulers and religious people came to India during its early history. Alexander the Great, the powerful Greek conqueror, came to India in 326 B.C. He was followed by the Scythians and the Arabs. An important group, the Guptas, built an empire which lasted from A.D. 320 to about A.D. 500. The Guptas made advances in medicine, art, and education. Cities of great wealth and beauty, along with universities, came into being during this time.

The Great Mogul Empire

The word *Mogul* meant "Mongol" in the Indian language. It first referred to the famous Genghis Khan, a Mongolian conqueror of the twelfth and thirteenth centuries. He was a **forebear** of the Mogul rulers.

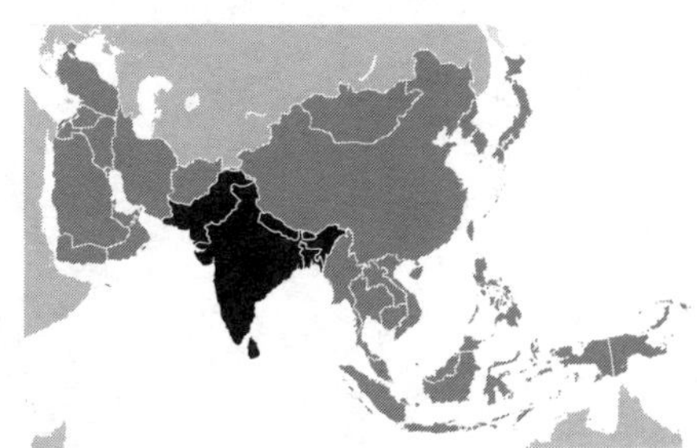

Chapter 6 – India

Words to Know

viceroy:
person who rules a country or province, acting as the king's or queen's representative

The first of the Great Mogul emperors was Babur, who came from Central Asia. His forces brought the Islamic religion to India. It is the second-largest religious group in India today. Miniature painting, literature, and art were also brought to India by Asian people. Akbar is considered the greatest of the Moguls. He ruled at the same time that Elizabeth I ruled England. He had more subjects and greater wealth than she did. The famous Taj Mahal was built by the Shah Jahan, another Mogul ruler. It was built as a tomb for his favorite wife. Later he was buried there. Today, it is considered to be one of the most beautiful buildings in the world.

The last of the great Mogul rulers, Aurangzeb, died in 1707. The great empire passed on to other hands. The influence of the Mogul empire can still be seen in the culture of India today.

The Taj Mahal is India's most famous building.

The British East India Company Begins Trading with India

Europeans began coming to India when spices and other things of value were discovered. The first explorer was the famous Portuguese Vasco da Gama, who came to India at about the same time that Columbus discovered America. Many European countries fought for control of the ports on India's west coast.

In 1600 a group of British traders obtained permission from Queen Elizabeth I to trade with India. These traders became known as the British East India Company. They became the most successful of all the European traders. At first, this company was only interested in acquiring the spices of India. However, the company later obtained land and began taxing the Indian people.

Some of the Indian princes would not accept the rule of the British East India Company. A great rebellion was staged by the princes. They lost the battle, and Great Britain took complete control. Other parts of India made agreements with Great Britain to be supervised by them. These areas became Indian states, ruled by the princes. The British head of the Indian government was known as a **viceroy**. The Indian states promised loyalty to the viceroy. In return, the states were protected by Great Britain. Great Britain helped to defend the Indians in wars against other countries. Great Britain also helped to modernize India by building railroads, telephone systems, irrigation systems, and factories.

LESSON REVIEW

Directions: Number your paper from 1 to 5. Then answer the following questions.

1. Which Mogul ruler brought the Islamic religion to India?
2. Why was the British East India Company formed and how did it change in its purpose?
3. Write the following events in the order that they occurred:

   Alexander the Great came to India.

   The Taj Mahal was built by Shah Jahan.

   Guptas made advances in medicine and art.
4. Why do you think Great Britain agreed to the formation of the Indian states ruled by princes?
5. How did Great Britain help India?

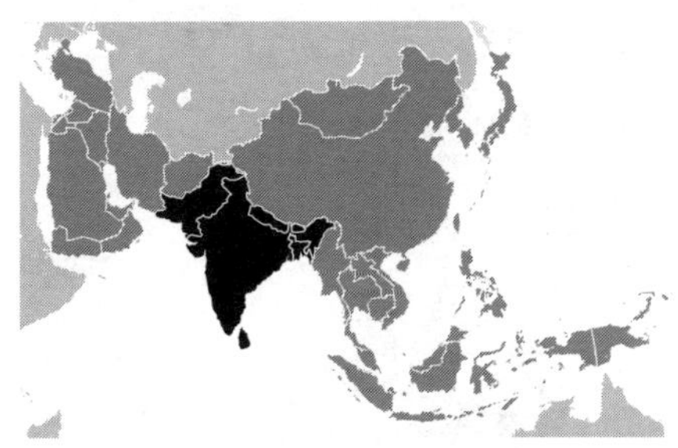

LESSON 3: India's Struggle to Become an Independent Country

Words to Know

assassinate:
to murder a famous person by secret attack

boycott:
to join together as a group and refuse to do or buy something

massacre:
the cruel killing of large numbers of people or animals

Just as the American colonies wanted their freedom from Great Britain and fought for their independence, India had wanted independence since the 1800s. Great Britain recognized this fact and formed the Indian National Congress to speak for the people. It was made up of Indian representatives.

India tried to pass some reforms. One reform appointed Indian leaders to assist the viceroy by serving on an advisory council. Despite these efforts by England, the unrest continued and even brought about acts of violence. After World War I, many Indians thought that they would receive more control of their own land.

A turning point in this struggle was a **massacre** of Indians by the British. The British fired on a group of unruly and unarmed Indians. More than 400 were killed, and many more wounded. This incident made the Indians even more determined to win complete independence.

Independence Finally Comes to India

During World War II, India helped the British by making war supplies and producing agricultural products. Air bases and troop training bases were set up in India. In return for this support, Britain assured India that it would be given independence after the war.

Throughout the war, Britain worked to solve the problems between the Hindus and Muslims. Despite all efforts, the fighting continued. In August of 1946 a riot occurred between the two groups. Many people were killed. Great Britain realized that the only way to solve the problem was to agree to the Muslim request for their own country. Therefore, Pakistan was separated from India and given to the Muslims. India then became a country of mostly Hindus. Pakistan was further divided into two areas—West Pakistan and East Pakistan. East Pakistan later became the country of Bangladesh.

The creation of the two separate countries did not bring an end to the conflict. Fighting continued, and many villages were destroyed and people killed. The northern state of Kashmir was invaded by Pakistan because many Muslims lived there. In order to protect itself, Kashmir became a part of India. The fighting over Kashmir continues even though the United Nations stepped in and called for a cease-fire.

In 1948 a great spiritual leader of India, Mohandas Gandhi, was **assassinated**. This act was done by a Hindu who resented Gandhi's beliefs. Gandhi believed every person had worth, even the Muslims and the untouchables, who are the lowest caste of people.

Mohandas K. Gandhi

Mohandas K. Gandhi was known as *Mahatma,* which means "great man." He was an Indian lawyer who gave himself totally to the independence movement. After the terrible killing of 400 unarmed Indians, Gandhi convinced many Indian people to use nonviolent acts against the British. Some of these acts included refusing to pay taxes, **boycotting** English schools, and refusing to obey British laws. He also encouraged the Indians to refuse to work for the British. His nonviolent movement began with a few people but it grew to include millions. Gandhi's methods also proved to be a powerful force against the British. Many people consider him to be a holy man.

What Type of Government Does India Have?

When India became a democratic republic in 1947, Jawaharlal Nehru became its first prime minister. Nehru was a firm believer in Gandhi's ideas. New Delhi became the capital of India. Under Nehru's guidance, India wrote a constitution much like the United States Constitution. According to India's constitution, each person has basic equal rights. There is a supreme court as well as lower courts in all the states of India. Laws for India are made by a parliament similar to the one in Great Britain. The elected members represent the 25 states and 7 territories of India.

Although the states have their own governors to rule them, the federal government of India is very powerful. It does not recognize the same states' rights as the United States does. Unlike our federal government, it can make changes in the constitution without the approval of the states. For example, it can change the boundaries of the states and even make new states. Most tax money collected in India goes to the federal government. This situation makes each state very dependent on the federal government.

Voting in India

In the United States only about half of the eligible voters vote. In India, most people vote in the national and state elections. Many of these people cannot read and write, so simple ballots using party symbols are used. The voter simply puts an "x" on the symbol representing the party of his or her choice and puts the ballot in a ballot box. India holds the largest democratic elections in the world. Throughout India's 25 states, there are many political parties but only four national parties.

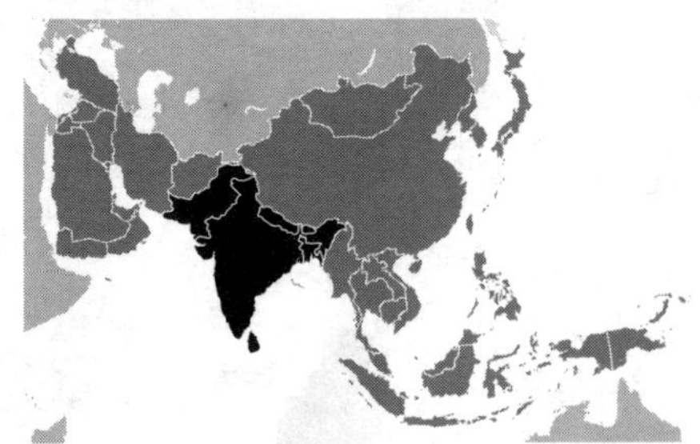

This man, a member of the Sikh religious group, is casting his vote.

The Congress Party is one of the most popular national parties. Indira Gandhi, Nehru's daughter, was a member of this party. She was prime minister from 1966 to 1977. She was defeated in the election of 1976 and remained out of power for three years. In 1980, Indira Gandhi was re-elected. She was assassinated in 1984. The assassin was a member of a group that felt that India had passed unfair laws. Gandhi's son, Rajiv Gandhi, was then elected prime minister. He was also a member of the Congress Party. He was killed by terrorists in 1991. To this day, India's political leaders do not travel outside the government buildings or their homes without bodyguards.

LESSON REVIEW

Directions: Number your paper from 1 to 4. Then answer the following questions.

1. How did India help Great Britain during World War II?
2. Why were West and East Pakistan created?
3. Compare and contrast India's government to that of the United States.
4. Why do you think Indians are more interested in voting than Americans are?

LESSON 4: The People of India

The more than one billion people who live in India belong to many different races. More than 1,000 languages and dialects are spoken in this country. These differences make communication difficult in a country the size of India, which is only about one-third as large as the United States. The states of India were divided according to the spoken language. How would you feel if you went to a neighboring state in the United States and could not understand the language? To help solve India's language problem, the government made Hindi the official language. English is used for official international communication.

Hinduism and Islam Are the Main Religions of India

More than 80 percent of the Indian people are Hindus, and only about 12 percent are Muslims. Although Hindu temples exist throughout India, most Hindus worship at home, where a special place is set aside for meditation. Hindus believe in many gods. The three gods of the Hindu myths are Brahma, who creates; Shiva, who destroys; and Vishnu, who preserves. Shiva and Vishnu are still worshiped by the Indians, although Brahma is not. Every aspect of a Hindu's life is affected by a religious belief. For example, one belief discourages the killing and eating of animals. Cows are considered sacred and are not used for food. Some animals, such as the water buffalo, help with farming, but many animals are allowed to roam freely.

Although not all Indians are Hindus, India's culture is influenced by this religion. The rapid population growth in India has, in part, been a result of the Hindu belief that having large families is a sign of goodness. Hindus believe it is the duty of people to have children. Water has a special place in the Hindu religion. Hindus bathe often and consider the waters of some rivers to be holy. People travel many miles to the great rivers of India to purify themselves in the holy waters. The Ganges River is considered the holiest of all the rivers.

Islam, the religion of the Muslims, is the second-largest religion in India today. The Muslims are the followers of Muhammad. They believe in one god, Allah. Their sacred book is called the Koran. Most Muslims begin studying the Koran at about age seven. The Hindus of India treat the Muslims as a separate group in the caste system. There are also several smaller religious groups in India. The Sikhs, who are often soldiers, have combined some ideas from both the Hindu and Muslim religion. Many wear turbans on their heads. Jains, Buddhists, and Christians also live in India. Most Christians live in the Kerala state on the west coast of India.

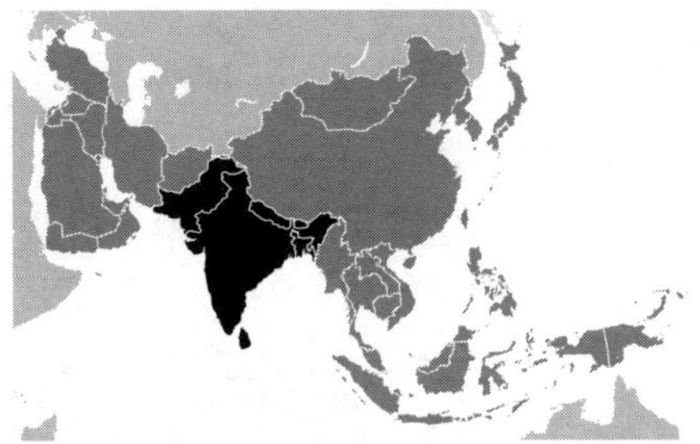

Words to Know

surplus:
an amount that is left over

The caste system, a Hindu belief, has been followed by most Indians. Today, this system is less strict than it once was. According to the Hindu religion, all people were grouped by the caste system. In this system, the birth of people into certain groups determined their worth. According to this system, there are four *varna*, or main classes. The highest caste of priests, or Brahmans, is considered to be the purest. The rulers and warriors are next in line, followed by traders and professionals. The farm laborers and servants are lower than the traders and professionals. Lowest is a group of people known as the untouchables, who are outside the caste system.

People of different castes usually did not marry or even associate with each other. All social life in India was based on the caste system. Hindus belonged to the caste of their parents, and they could not leave it. All the people of one caste did the same work.

More and more, educated people in the cities ignore the caste system. They marry anyone they choose. They work at jobs outside of their caste. The president of India in 1997 was a member of the untouchable class. There is also a member of India's Supreme Court who was born an untouchable and grew up on the streets. However, most of the people living in villages in the rural areas still follow the caste system. One useful thing this system has done is to help preserve the special skills and crafts of the people.

LESSON REVIEW

Directions: Number your paper from 1 to 5. Then answer the following questions.

1. How were the states of India divided?
2. What percent of the people are Hindus and what percent are Muslims? What other religions are found in India?
3. Name some ways in which the Hindu religion affects daily lives of people.
4. Why do you think that many people in India no longer accept the caste system?
5. Why do you think water is considered holy by many Indians?

LESSON 5: Life in the Villages of India

Life in the villages centers around farming. Farm people have been living, working, marrying, and raising their children in the same way for thousands of years.

The people of the villages are poor. About one-third of them own the land they farm. The money they make on the crops they grow is used to pay rent for the land. Because many of them are so poor, they cannot afford chemical fertilizer, modern equipment, or good seeds. Many families are poorly fed, and their diets contain little protein. Religious beliefs prevent them from eating meat.

The fields lie outside the farming villages. Members of the family work together in the fields. Water buffaloes are used to pull the plows. Much of the other work is done by hand. The crops are usually of poor quality because of the lack of fertilizer. Other problems faced by farmers in many parts of India are droughts and floods. Only some parts of India have irrigation systems to provide water for the farmers during a drought.

Farming Improvements

During the 1960s, some important steps were taken by the government to improve farming. This period became known as the Green Revolution. New types of wheat and rice seed were given to farmers. This new seed produced more rice and wheat per acre. Fertilizer was offered for sale at a price that farmers could afford. Farmers were also educated in the use of modern machinery. In some areas these improvements worked well. For the first time in India's history a **surplus** of wheat and rice was produced. This surplus allowed crops to be stored for times of famine. New crops have also been introduced in India—corn and soybeans.

These children are pumping water from a local water pump.

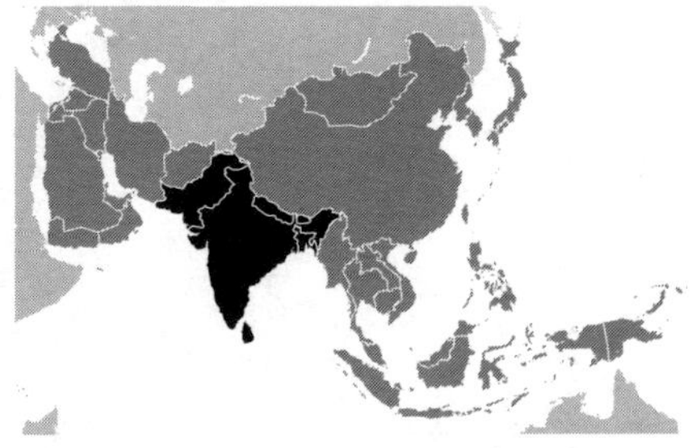

Soybeans have become a great source of protein to the Indians, who eat little or no meat. Some babies are now fed soybean milk. There is even a soft drink made from soybeans!

A Different Way of Life in the Cities of India

Even though most of the Indian people work at farming and live in villages, some Indians live and work in the cities. In the modern cities, businessmen dress in suits and ties. There are factories, apartment houses, restaurants, movie theaters, hotels, and stores. In the cities of India, the new and old ways of living can be seen. Modern cars and buffalo carts travel on the same city streets. Indians dressed in *saris*, a traditional Indian costume, can be seen riding on modern buses and trains. The number of people moving to the cities is growing each year. Overcrowding is becoming a serious problem. Slum areas are growing because many people who move to the cities cannot find work.

Most industries can be found in and near the large cities of the country. Bombay, now called Mumbai, is one of Asia's busiest ports. It has large textile mills. The government provides incentives for textiles to be manufactured. Iron and steel mills are found in and around Calcutta. India produces enough iron ore to sell to the world market. India's other growing businesses are engineering and manufacturing of machinery, chemicals, and cement. Recently, India has become one of the world's largest producers of computer software.

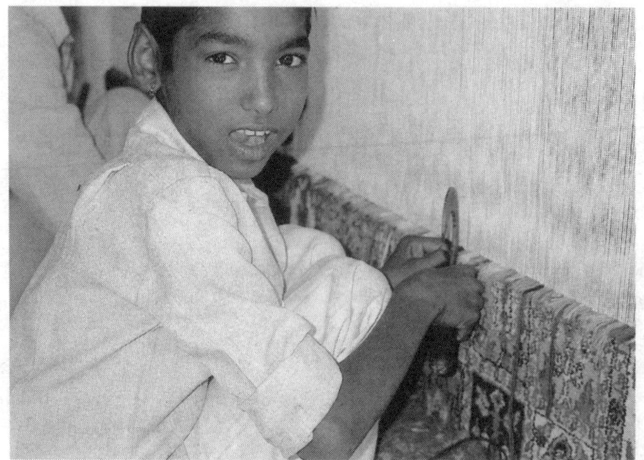

It's not unusual to find children working in factories in India. This boy in Jaipur, India, is weaving a carpet.

Production of Village Crafts Is Encouraged

Not all the people who come to the cities can find work. Unemployment and overcrowding are major problems. The government wants people to stay in their villages until the factories expand enough to offer more jobs. One way it helps people remain in the villages is to encourage them to produce handmade goods.

Indian people have always been excellent artists. Specialized skills have been handed down from generation to generation. Modern people still follow ancient traditions and create a variety of products. They make beautiful silver objects, jewelry, carpets, and pottery. The major exported crafts include hand-knotted woolen carpets, hand-printed textiles, leather goods, and wooden and cane ware.

These women in Jodhpur, India, are decorating clay pots.

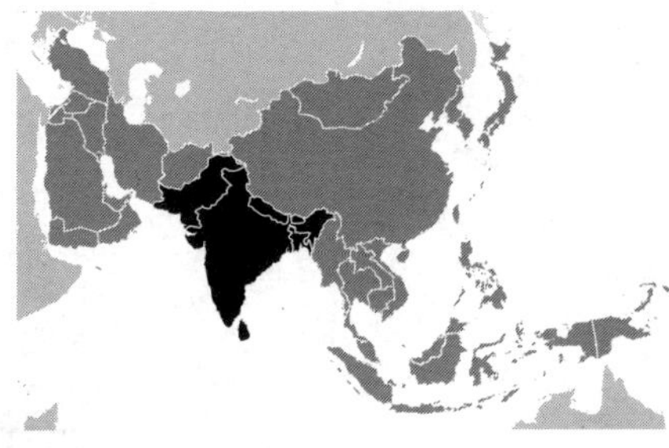

Words to Know

dowry:
money or property a woman brings to the man she marries

The New Economy of India

In 1991 the government of India started programs to improve India's economy. Trade with other countries increased. The United States became India's main trading partner. American businesses opened in India. This provided more opportunities to young Indian workers.

Despite these new developments, there is still great poverty in India. Thousands of poor people live here in houses made from cinder blocks or matting. They use the Jamuna River in Bangladesh for washing clothes, bathing, and cooking.

India is now one of the top five countries in software production. The software industry is making a small number of people very wealthy. Yet only 50 miles away, there are villages where poor families work in the fields for about 50 cents a day.

Illiteracy is common, and there is little communication with the outside world. Some villages have only one telephone that works.

The new industries are not providing enough money for the Indian government to close the gap between the wealthy and the poor. This, along with the old rules of the caste system, keep the poor people of India from improving their lives.

LESSON REVIEW

Directions: Number your paper from 1 to 5. Then answer the following questions.

1. What are some reasons farming was difficult in India?
2. What types of industries are found in India?
3. Explain the Green Revolution. How have soybeans become important?
4. Do you think that the government will succeed in keeping people in the villages? Explain your answer.
5. How do you think that India will solve problems such as overcrowding and lack of employment in the cities?

LESSON 6: The Family Life of the Indian People

The members of Indian families are very close, and their families live together. Traditional families live according to the old way—a husband, wife, children, and the married sons and their families—all live together. Older daughters who are not married live with their families. Married daughters live with their husband's families. Marriages are often arranged, which means the parents of the bride choose a husband for her. They also provide a **dowry** for the bride and groom.

The traditional, or extended, type of family still exists for a number of reasons. Often the members of these families work at the same type of job. If they are all farmers, the extended family provides many people to help on the land. If they are merchants, family members can share ideas and money to improve business. Many people feel that it is safer to live in a large family group. The head of the traditional family is the oldest male. He makes the main decisions, especially those involving money. The oldest female is in charge of the household. The men associate mostly with the other men, and the women stay with the other women. Children are important in these large households. They are cared for by all members of the family.

Not all families in India follow traditional family practices. Some people choose to live apart from their parents when they marry. Modern families are found mainly in the cities. Some city families still cling to the old traditional style of living, but many families are breaking up. Since it is difficult to find work in the city, family members may not have the same type of job or they earn different wages. This situation makes sharing the income difficult. The working members are not always willing to support the unemployed, and the family breaks up.

These elementary students attend school in a small Indian village.

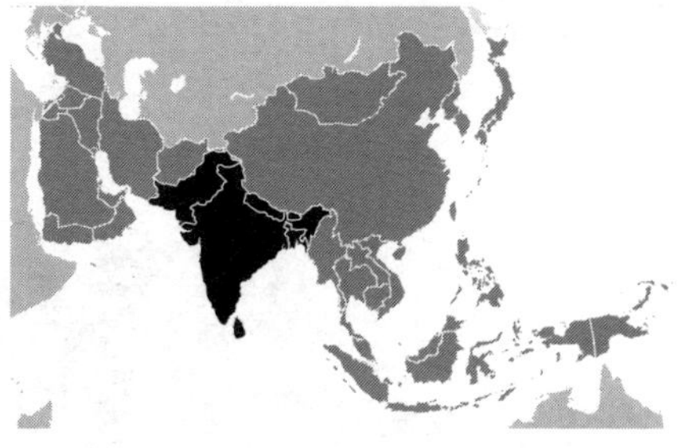

CHAPTER 6 – INDIA

Words to Know

literate:
having the ability to read and write

Education in India

Before the government controlled education, about 80 percent of the population could not read or write. In the Hindu villages, the children were educated by religious leaders, especially children in the higher castes. Muslims were educated at the mosques. Elementary schools were provided for all levels of castes except the untouchables. Some high schools existed, and wealthy people had tutors for their children.

After India's independence, many more children were educated. Today about 50 percent of the schools are privately run by religious groups. Most schools start at the elementary level, not at the kindergarten level as they do in our country. In addition to reading and writing, children learn crafts, such as weaving and pottery-making. Students are taught in the language of the area where they live. Some are also taught Hindi. After completing high school, students must take examinations. These tests decide if students will go to college or will take a job. They take another test after the second year of college to see if they should continue. India has many technical schools to prepare students for jobs in mechanics, teaching, farming, and business.

Many more Indians are **literate** because of the government's effort to improve education. However, it is difficult to find teachers for the villages. Many poor people do not receive an education. Children are not required by law to go to school, as they are in the United States and many other countries. If children are needed at home to work on the farms, their parents will not send them to school.

Recreation

Cities offer many leisure activities including games, sports, music, and dance. A favorite recreation among all Indians is going to the movies. Theaters are usually crowded even though videos can be used at home. India produces as many movies as Japan and United States. Some other types of recreation found in the cities are enjoyed only by the wealthy. Examples include concerts, plays, and horse racing.

Cricket is played by adults and children alike. Polo, a sport that began in India, is enjoyed by the more wealthy people. Badminton also originated in India. Young people enjoy many games and sports both in and out of school. They have school teams for cricket, field hockey, and basketball. After school, they practice for competition with other teams. At school, the students have physical training.

Some sports have developed in the villages. Among these games is wrestling. The style and rules vary from village to village. Sports involving animals are also popular. These activities include horse riding events, an Indian version of the bullfight, and both camel and elephant races.

Yoga, with its special exercises and mind control, is practiced by many Indians and other people all over the world. Many games that originated in India are enjoyed worldwide, such as chess.

The Arts in India

Some of the finest examples of India's architecture can be found in its religious buildings. Ruins of these buildings still remain; they date to 200 B.C. Old Hindu temples, with their distinctive towers, can be seen throughout India. The blocks used to build the temples tell stories of the gods.

The religious art of the Muslims was brought to India when the country was invaded by the Moguls. Their places of worship, called mosques, often show the art of inlaying semiprecious stones and marble. This art can be seen at its finest in the famous Taj Mahal in Agra (see picture on page 114). Miniature painting, which originated in Iran, then called Persia, was popular at the time of the Mogul rulers. This painting on small pieces of paper showed mainly the life among the higher classes. The Buddhists developed a form of wall painting that was done in caves.

The Indian dance system is among the oldest in the world.

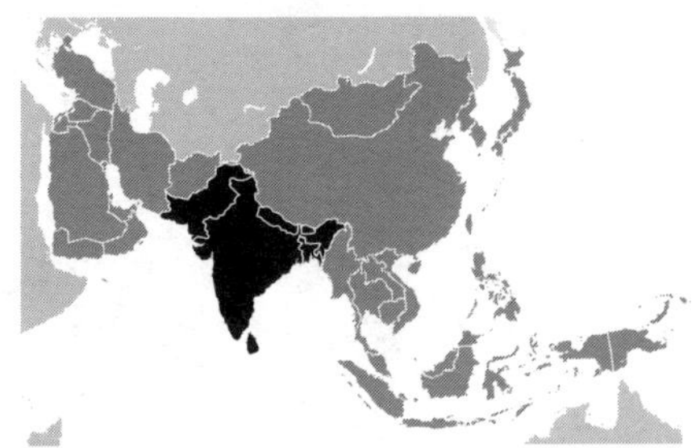

Traditional Indian music sounds different from Western music. It can be heard at weddings, concerts, and festivals. String instruments, called sitars, are used in addition to flutes and drums. This type of music also accompanies Indian dancers. The classical dances tell stories of Hindu gods and heroes. Moods are shown by the body positions of the dancers and the way in which they move their hands and arms. Both music and dance are related to religious beliefs.

LESSON REVIEW

Directions: Number your paper from 1 to 5. Then answer the following questions.

1. Describe traditional family life in India. Why does it still exist?
2. What is a favorite recreation among Indians?
3. Where can examples of Indian architecture be found?
4. Why are city families not following traditional ways of living? Do you think this change will happen in rural areas? Why or why not?
5. What can India's government do to improve education? Do you think other countries should help India? Why or why not?

Spotlight Story

Food in the Cities and Villages

The largest meal of the week is served on Sunday afternoon. This is a time when the family gathers together. The meal may start with cabbage soup, followed by a rice dish. *Chapatti*, a round, flat wheat cake, is used as bread. Sometimes chapattis are filled with meat and vegetables. To end this special meal, a final course of yogurt and fruit may be served. During the week, the typical meal is smaller. It consists of rice, one or two vegetables, a bit of fish or meat, and chapattis. Indian families seldom use forks. They pick up the food with their fingertips or with pieces of chapatis. Favorite fruits are pomegranates, pineapples, and large purple grapes. Curry dishes are also a favorite in India. These dishes are very spicy. Curry is usually used with meat or fish, tomatoes, onions, garlic, and spices.

Kela ka Rayta

(Yogurt with Banana and Coconut)

Ingredients:
2 T. butter
1 t. black mustard seeds
1/2 c. grated coconut
1 t. salt
1 c. plain yogurt
1 medium banana cut into 1/4″ slices
1 t. finely chopped coriander

Directions: In a small skillet, heat the butter. Drop in mustard seeds and heat until they begin to burst; add the coconut. Stir, remove from skillet, and add 2 T. of yogurt. Place remaining yogurt in a bowl and stir in the mixture from the skillet. Add the banana, coriander, and salt and toss gently. Refrigerate for one hour, tightly covered, before serving.

SPOTLIGHT REVIEW

Answer the following questions.

1. When is the week's largest meal served?
2. What are chapattis?
3. Describe a typical weekly meal.
4. Describe how Indians eat their food.
5. What is a popular spice in India?

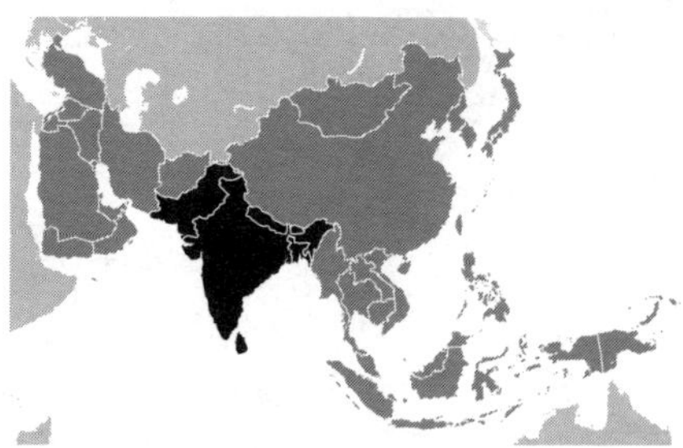

Chapter 6 Review

The first Indians lived in the Indus valley and had a well-developed civilization. This civilization weakened as invaders came to conquer India. Around the year 1600, Europeans came to India and formed a trading company called the British East India Trading Company. This move led to almost complete British control of India for many years. It was not until 1947, after years of struggle, that India became an independent nation.

Today, India is a democratic republic with a prime minister and a parliament. There are 25 states with their own governments. The people of India are mostly Hindus. Their entire culture, with its customs and traditions, is based on the Hindu religion. India's architecture includes beautiful temples and mosques. The most famous is the Taj Mahal. Poetry has always been enjoyed by Indians, especially long epic poems that tell stories.

Critical Thinking Skills

Directions: Think about the questions below. Be sure to answer in complete sentences.

1. How is India's government similar to the government of the United States? How is it different?
2. What do you think is the major reason that 80 percent of the Indians are Hindus? Whose life do you think is easier—a Hindu's or a Muslim's?
3. Give reasons why you think that the illiteracy rate has gone down in India in recent years.
4. Compare the actions of Gandhi and his followers to the actions taken by Martin Luther King Jr. and his followers.
5. Why do you think that family life in India is changing? Will this change help the economy? Explain your answer.

For Discussion

1. In your opinion, why is India the world's largest movie-making country? Why do you think movies are so popular in such a poor country?
2. If you could help the poor of India, what are some things you would do? What are some ways in which the Indians might help themselves?
3. What are some signs of British influence in India today?
4. How do you think the growing industries will help the future economy and general welfare of the people?
5. Why do you think that some Indians feel it is important to maintain the caste system? Do you think the caste system will hold back or help India's developing economy?

Write It!

Directions: Research the life of Gandhi, Nehru, or other important figures in India's struggle for independence. Write a report that includes all aspects of this person's life (childhood, education, family, occupations). Explain how this person has affected life in India today.

For You To Do

Directions: Invite a person who is a native of India to class. This person could discuss his or her occupation, reasons for living in the United States, and things they like or dislike about both countries.

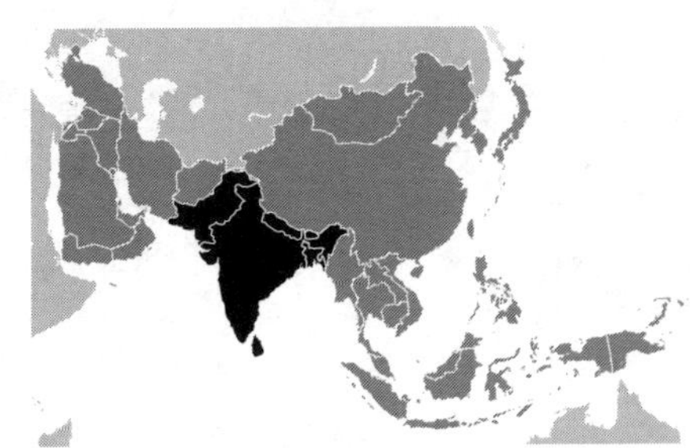

MIDDLE EAST

CHAPTER 7

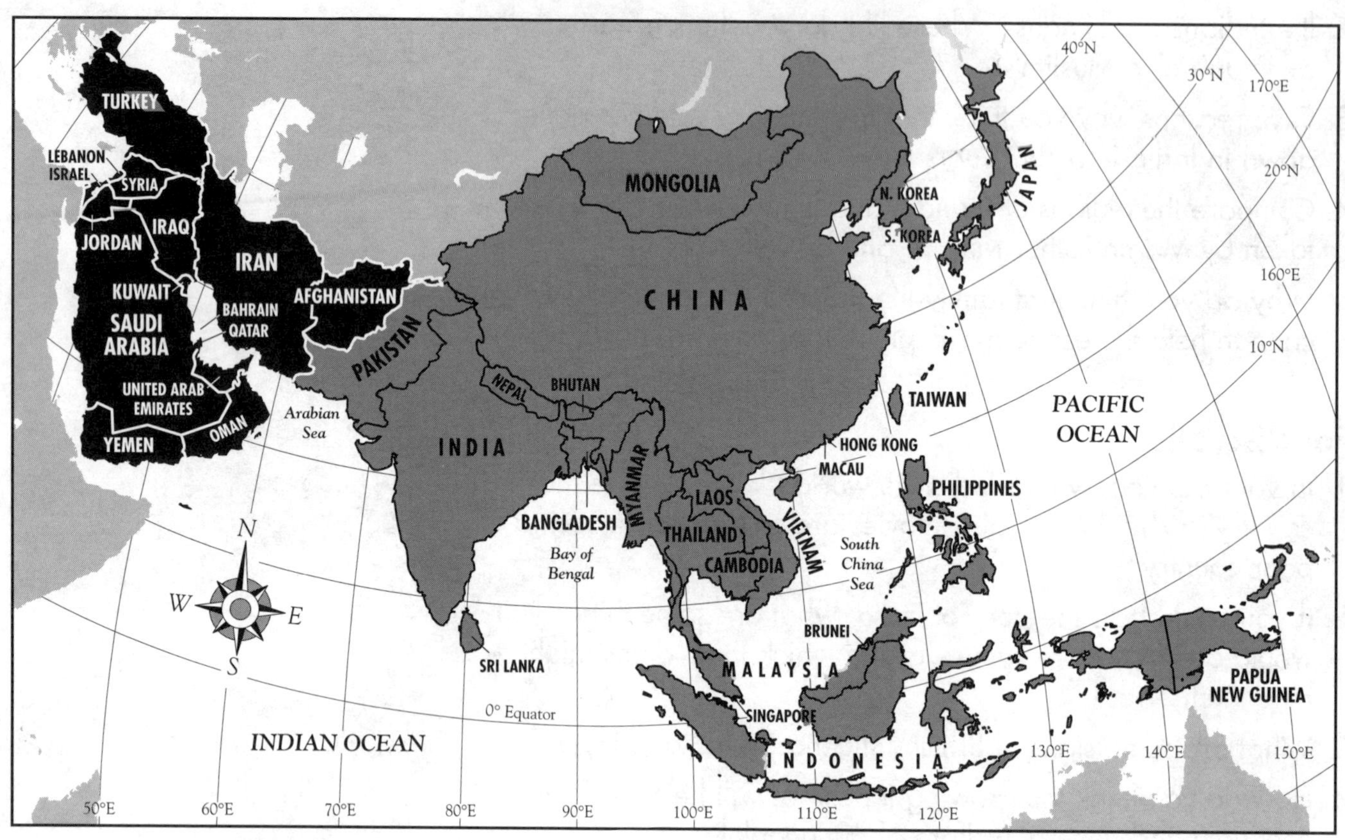

Fast Facts

- The Middle East is located where Asia, Europe, and Africa meet.
- The countries along the Persian Gulf are leaders in oil production.
- The first great civilizations developed in the Middle East.
- Judaism, Christianity, and Islam had their beginnings in this area.

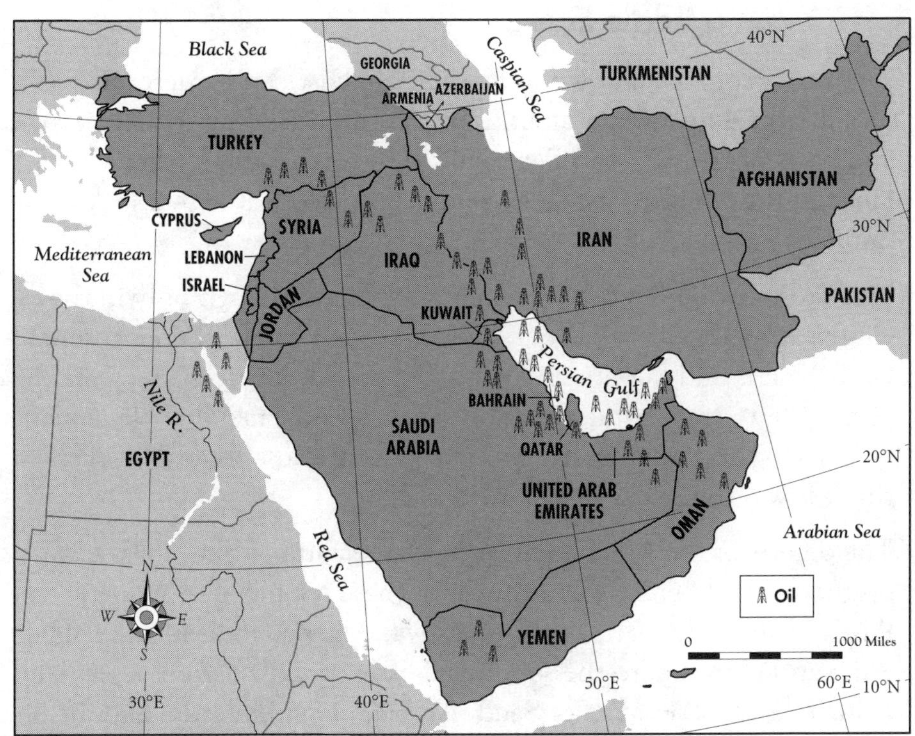

MAP SKILLS

Oil Fields and Pipelines

The oil found in the Middle East is valuable. It is carried by pipelines from the oil fields to seaports. The oil is then shipped to countries throughout the world.

Directions: Study the map above to answer these questions.

1. Which country that borders the Black Sea has oil fields?
2. Which country has the most oil fields?
3. Which countries have no oil fields?
4. Some oil is found in land under water. Which body of water has oil fields under it?

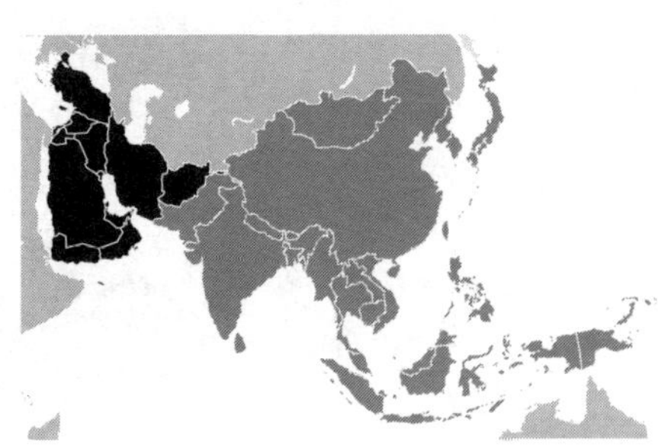

Words to Know

dune:
a mound or ridge of loose sand heaped up by the wind

LESSON 1: The Geography and Climate of the Middle East

The region of Asia known as the Middle East can be described as flat, hot, and dry. Some mountains exist in Turkey, northern Iran, and parts of the Arabian Peninsula and the Sahara. However, the lands of the Middle East share one distinctive feature—a lack of rainfall.

One area that does receive adequate rainfall, although only in the winter, is the Fertile Crescent. This V-shaped fertile plain is formed by the Tigris and Euphrates Rivers. The Fertile Crescent includes parts of Iran, Iraq, Syria, Lebanon, Jordan, and Israel. People have been living and farming in this area for centuries. Some historians think it was the site of the Garden of Eden.

The deserts of the Middle East cover large parts of Iran, Jordan, and southern Israel. The Sahara is west of these countries in North Africa. It includes parts of Egypt, Libya, Algeria, and Morocco. The Arabian Peninsula, to the south, is mostly dry and barren desert land. It includes the countries of Saudi Arabia, Qatar, Bahrain, Kuwait, United Arab Emirates, Oman, South Yemen, and Yemen. A huge, barren area in the southern part of the Arabian Peninsula is known as the Empty Quarter. It is about the size of Texas and is made up of salt flats and sand **dunes**. Very few people go there except wandering nomads. Although the Middle East is an area of deserts and mountains, it is not cut off from the rest of the world. The Middle East connects Europe to Asia. Throughout history, famous leaders, traders, and nomadic people have traveled through the lands of the Middle East.

Deserts Are Not All Sand

You may think that a desert is made up of only sand and sand dunes. Although many people think so, this view is not entirely correct. Some of the desert is flat and sandy, but most of it contains bare rock, small pebbles, and sandstone. There are also mountains and high peaks in some places.

Deserts are also thought to be hot all the time. During the day, the hot, tropical sun bakes the sand and bare rock. However, at night the temperature on the desert drops. In some places the temperature goes below 40°F.

The Climate of the Middle East Is Hot and Dry

The Middle East is mainly a region of deserts. The climate of the area is hot and dry most of the time. The hot sun, the constant winds, and the lack of rainfall make living in or near the deserts difficult. Summers are very hot, and the skies are always clear. The scarcity of water has always been a problem. Sometimes several years go by without rain. In some parts of the desert, oases form around springs and wells. An oasis is an area with enough water to support plants and people. The rivers are another source of water.

The people who came to the Middle East settled near the rivers and the oases. When these areas became crowded, the people moved away from these moist lands. It took many people to dig irrigation ditches to carry water to farm fields. It was necessary for villagers to help one another get water to their crops. Today the people use modern methods of irrigation. Dams are built to hold the water. Some water must be processed from sea water into fresh water. This process is very expensive.

Although most of the Middle East is dry, the lands along the Mediterranean Sea have a more pleasant climate. It is much like the climate of California in the United States. The summers are long and hot, but the winters are mild with some rainfall. Because of this climate, more crops are grown in the lands along the Mediterranean Sea. Olives and grapes are grown on the hillsides. Oranges, lemons, and figs are plentiful in most of the area. In the lowlands and hills, people raise sheep and goats because there is enough grass for the herds.

LESSON REVIEW

Directions: Number your paper from 1 to 5. Then answer the following questions.

1. Where are the desert areas of the Middle East located? What is the Empty Quarter?
2. Describe what a desert is really like.
3. Why do you think the Fertile Crescent is an important area in the Middle East?
4. If you visited areas near the Mediterranean Sea, what types of work would you see the people doing?
5. How have the governments of some countries solved the problems related to climate? What else do you think can be done?

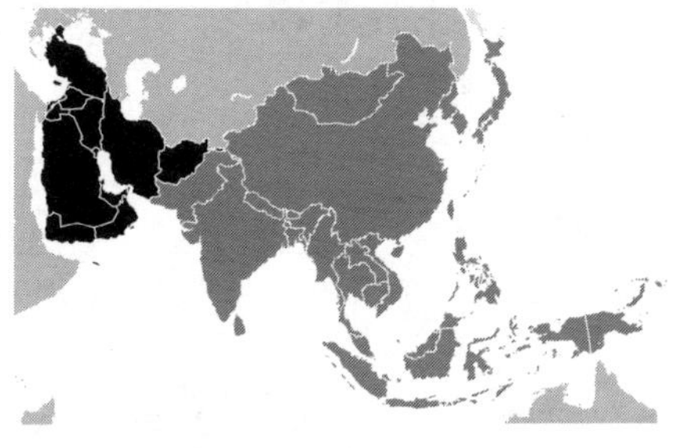

LESSON 2: The History of the Middle East

Historians agree that the Middle East was among the first areas where civilization began. Two civilizations developed at the same time. One was in Egypt, and the other was in what is now Iraq. The ancient Egyptians lived along the Nile River in Africa. About 800 miles away in Mesopotamia (now Iraq), the Sumerians developed a civilization near the Tigris and Euphrates Rivers.

These two great civilizations were at war for many years. Both had powerful governments and a ruling class. The Sumerians built a canal system to help irrigate their land for farming. They also created a system of writing.

The Middle East had continuous fighting. New civilizations took control, one after the other. The Jewish people, led by Moses, escaped slavery in Egypt and set up a kingdom along the Mediterranean Sea in what is now Israel. King Solomon, their ruler, built a great temple in the city of Jerusalem. Other strong groups then conquered the area and drove out the Jewish people. The Persians were the next group to control much of the Mediterranean region. The Persian Empire included Iran, the eastern Mediterranean lands, and Egypt. It allowed the Jewish people to return to their homeland, Israel.

This man is praying at the Wailing Wall in Jerusalem, Israel.

Alexander the Great and the Romans Were Next to Rule the Area

Alexander the Great, from the European country of Macedonia, conquered the Middle East next. His empire included all the lands from Greece to India. He introduced the Greek language to these areas. After his death, the people of his empire began fighting with one another. The Romans then conquered Alexander's empire and sent the Jewish people from their homeland once again. The empire then became known as the Byzantine Empire. This empire was constantly at war with the rulers of what is now Iraq, Iran, and Afghanistan. However, neither side won.

The Arabs and Islam Become Powerful in the Middle East

A third group, the Arabs on the Arabian Peninsula, was rising in power. The Arab people lived in tribes. Some tribes were Christians, and others worshipped many gods. During the sixth century, Muhammad was born into one of the more powerful tribes. He believed in only one god, Allah, and founded the Islam religion based on this belief.

At first, many Arabs did not believe Muhammad. After moving to the city of Medina, he convinced many Arabs to follow his teachings. Within a few years, Muhammad united all the tribes of the area under the Islamic religion. They controlled the region until Muhammad' s death.

Other Invaders in the Middle East

After Muhammad' s death, many conflicts took place within the Muslim lands. Many groups gained control over the years. For two centuries, the region was invaded by foreigners who were not Muslim. The Crusaders, European Christians, and the Mongol nomadic tribes all tried to dominate the Middle East.

The next important group to rule the Middle East was the Turkish Ottoman Empire. They reached their peak in the sixteenth century and then slowly declined. After World War I, the Greeks invaded Turkey and tried to reclaim the land. A young Turkish army officer, Mustafa Kemal (known as Kemal Atatürk), began a national movement to drive out the Greeks. His efforts worked. By 1923, he declared Turkey a republic and moved the capital to Ankara.

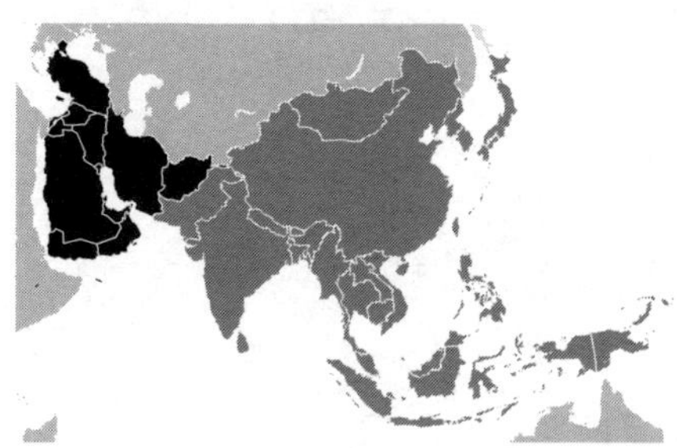

Words to Know

heritage:
traditions inherited or passed down from one generation to the next

imperialism:
control or influence a powerful nation has over a weaker country

isthmus:
a narrow strip of land connecting two larger land areas

sect:
a group of people that believe in the same religious ideas

European Control in the Middle East

In the eighteenth century, both England and France wanted to build a canal through the narrow Suez **isthmus**. This achievement would make shipping easier between Asia and Europe. The canal would connect the Mediterranean and Red Seas. France finished building the Suez Canal in 1869. It was owned by France, Turkey, and Egypt. (Egypt is part of Africa.) In 1875 Egypt sold its share of the canal to Britain. This change meant that Britain and France controlled the canal. Britain also gained control of nearby oil fields and approaches to the Suez Canal. France acquired land in North Africa.

Soon other European nations entered the struggle for land in the Middle East. Germany, Portugal, Belgium, and Spain eventually developed colonies. This control that powerful nations have over weaker countries is called **imperialism**. The nations that establishied colonies ususally had little respect for the native cultures of those colonies.

LESSON REVIEW

Directions: Number your paper from 1 to 5. Then answer the following questions.

1. What two great civilizations developed at the same time in the Middle East?
2. Write the following facts in the order they occurred in the history of the Middle East:

   the Arabs controlled the Middle East
   Moses led Jews to the Middle East
   France built the Suez Canal
   the Byzantine Empire took control
3. Who was Atatürk? Why was he important?
4. What is the importance of the Suez Canal?
5. Why do you think so many European nations became interested in acquiring lands in the Middle East?

LESSON 3: The People of the Middle East

Most of the people of the Middle East live near water sources. Almost half of the people of the Middle East are farmers. Some people make their living working in the cities.

Another small group of people who live in the Middle East are called nomads. Nomads travel from place to place to get food and water for their herds of animals. They live in tents and carry all of their possessions with them when they move. They may use camels or sometimes trucks to move from place to place.

Some Middle Eastern people have become extremely wealthy from the sale of oil. Oil is the most important natural resource in the Middle East. Huge reserves of oil were discovered in the Middle East in the 1950s.

About three-fourths of the people of the Middle East are Arabs and speak the Arabic language. In addition to Arabs, Turks, Iranians, Armenians, Kurds, and Israelis also live in this region. These groups are set apart by language, religion, and customs. More than 90 percent of the people of the Middle East are Muslims. Only two countries in the Middle East, Lebanon and Israel, follow other religions. About one-half of the Lebanese people are Christians, and the people of Israel are Jews.

The Turks and the Iranians

The Turks and the Iranians have lived in their own countries for hundreds of years. The Turks of today are 95 percent Muslims, and their language is Turkish. It is the most widely used language in the Middle East after Arabic. After World War I, Turkey was led by a strong leader named Kemal Atatürk. He modernized Turkey and was responsible for Turkish becoming the official language. He introduced modern methods of farming and gave women equal rights with men.

Today, many farmers in Turkey own their own farms. Turkey is considered one of the most modern countries in the Middle East. Many people wear Western-style clothes. In the cities people enjoy many forms of Western pastimes, such as movies and modern music.

Most Iranians are Muslims of the strict Shiite **sect**, but they are not Arabs. They trace their **heritage** back to the Aryans, a people who moved into the country 4,000 years ago. Their language is Farsi, a form of Arabic. Most of the people live together in farm villages to raise crops or livestock.

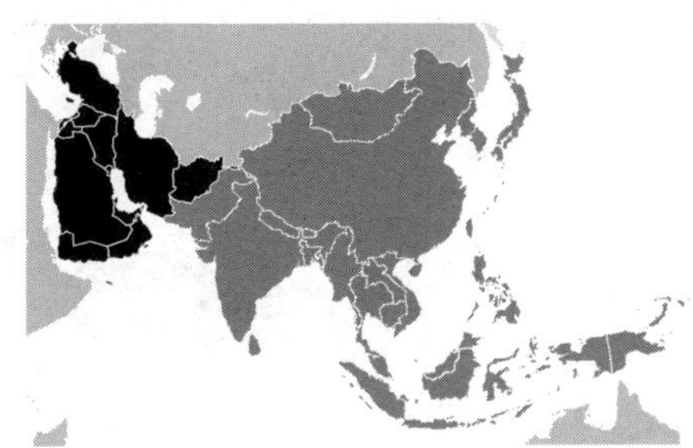

Words to Know

persecute:
to treat cruelly or unfairly, often for reasons of religious or political beliefs

Some Iranians work in the oil fields, oil refineries, or factories. Iran and some of its citizens have become wealthy because of the sale of oil in the past years.

Iran became more Westernized when many foreigners came into the country. Many Muslims were unhappy with the changes caused by Iran's wealth and blamed their leader, the shah of Iran. In 1979 he was overthrown and forced to flee the country. The new leader was the Ayatollah Khomeini. Iran was also at war with its neighbor, Iraq. Because of all the problems in Iran, the country lost some of its wealth.

The Israelis

The Israelis are bound together by the Jewish religion. They have had their own country since 1948. Israel was once called Palestine. It was the home of the Jewish people in biblical times. Through the years, the numbers of Jews living in Palestine decreased as the Arab population increased. After World War I, the Jews began to settle again in Palestine alongside the Arabs. During World War II, millions of Jews were murdered by the Nazis. Many fled to Palestine for safety. When the war ended, the United Nations created a new country for the Jewish people called Israel. The United States has supported Israel with money and weapons.

The people of Israel came from all parts of the world—Europe, the Americas, the Middle East, North Africa, and Asia. Muslims and Christians also live in Israel. Israel has a large army for protection against its Arab neighbors, some of whom still resent existence of the nation of Israel.

The Palestinians

Many of the Palestinians lost their homes and businesses when the United Nations created the nation of Israel. Most of the Arab nations did not recognize Israel as a nation, and conflicts broke out. Many people of Palestine were forced to flee their homes. They had to live in temporary camps because the Arab countries would not give them a new home. Some Palestinians remained in Israel, but they would not help the Israelis in their conflicts with the Arab countries.

Today, the Palestinians want to have their country back. Some Israelis do not think this is possible. Jews from all over the world are now living in Israel.

In 1964 the Palestinians created the Palestine Liberation Organization, or PLO, led by Yasser Arafat. The PLO is a group of people whose purpose is to protect the Palestinians living anywhere in the Middle East. The PLO wants Palestinians to have a country of their own alongside Israel. The PLO has received support, in the form of money and arms, from Arab states and from the former Soviet Union.

The Arabs

About three-fourths of the Middle Eastern people are Arabs. They are united by the Islamic religion and are called Muslims. All other groups—such as the Armenians, Iranians, Turks, Israelis, Palestinians, and Kurds—are minority groups living in the Middle East. The Arabic language is spoken by most Arabs, except in Turkey, Iran, and Afghanistan. The customs and way of life of the Arabs are greatly affected by their religion. During the rule of the ancient Arabs, many contributions to civilization were made.

The Arabs became known for their knowledge of science and mathematics. Scientists developed instruments to study the stars. They developed the system of Arabic numerals, including the zero. The basics of algebra were also developed. The word comes from the Arabic word, *algabar*. In medicine they studied the human body and ways to treat sickness. They identified the difference between measles and smallpox. The Arabs also translated Greek writings into Arabic.

The Armenians

The Armenians make up one of the largest minority groups in the Middle East. A hundred years ago, most made their homeland in a large section of Turkey. They had their own language, and most were Christians. The Armenians were **persecuted** in Turkey—in the late 1800s and again in the 1950s and 1960s. The Armenians fled to other countries and to Europe and America. Today, most live in Syria, Turkey, and Lebanon. Most Armenians are Christians.

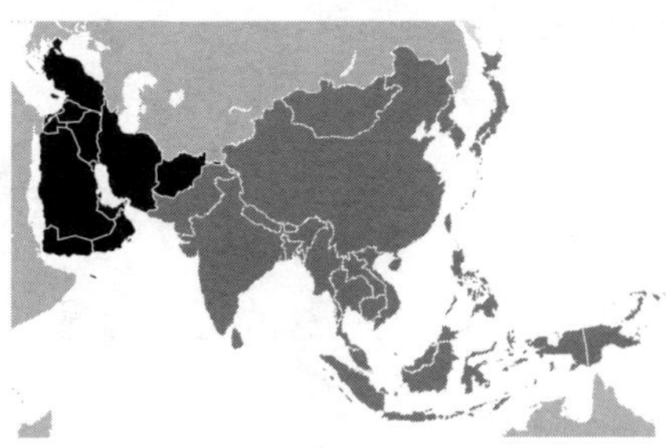

The Kurds

The Kurds are an independent minority group who follow the Muslim religion. They have their own distinct culture. They speak their own language, run their own schools, and wear their national costumes. About 25 million Kurds live in Turkey, Iraq, Iran, and Syria. They also have a desire for a homeland of their own and have fought for equal rights and local self-government in Iraq. The Kurds have rebelled several times in Iraq, although Iraq has been less harsh to them than other countries have been.

This Bedouin woman is carrying wood. The Bedouins are traditionally wanderers, but today many have settled in cities.

LESSON REVIEW

Directions: Number your paper from 1 to 5. Then answer the following questions.

1. What holds the Israelis together?
2. What is the PLO? What is its purpose?
3. What happened to Iran's leader in 1979?
4. What characteristics unite all of the Arabs of the Middle East?
5. Which contribution of the ancient Arab civilization do you think was the most important? Why?

LESSON 4: Life in Rural Areas of the Middle East

Most of the people living in the rural areas of the Middle East are farmers. Many live in very small villages. These villages are near a source of water or near an oasis. Only the modern villages have electricity. Some of the older, larger villages are built around a bazaar, which is a marketplace where goods are bought and sold. The bazaar also serves as a gathering place for the villagers. The bazaar may be near the village mosque in the Muslim countries.

The farm fields are located outside of the villages. Few farmers own their own land. The landowners supply them with water, tools, and farm animals in return for a share of the crops. In the countries of Jordan, Israel, Syria, Lebanon, and Turkey, the farmers depend on the rains to water the crops. The other countries with large desert areas depend on an irrigation system for water. They irrigate by using ditches, pipes, or tunnels to bring the water from rivers, streams, wells, or oases.

Large herds of sheep are raised in the Middle East. There is not enough grass for cattle. Herds of sheep almost always contain some goats. Both sheep and goats can eat low grass and roots. Some countries, such as Turkey, have set up programs to limit the amount of sheep herds because they can destroy so much of the vegetation, including young trees.

Farming Is Not Productive

The farmers of the desert areas are subsistence farmers. This means they raise only enough food to feed their own families. Everyone in the family works in the fields. In some areas the methods used by the farmers have not changed much since ancient times. Wooden plows are pulled by oxen or donkeys, and hand tools are used to harvest the crops. Animals are used to operate the pumps that bring water to the fields. The main crops grown are wheat, barley, millet, corn, and rice. Fruit is also grown in oasis areas.

The homes of the subsistence farmers are small and made of dried mud or brick. These families have few possessions. They usually sleep and eat on rugs or mats on the floor. The people do not eat much meat, except for lamb. The main foods are breads, goat cheese, fruits, and vegetables.

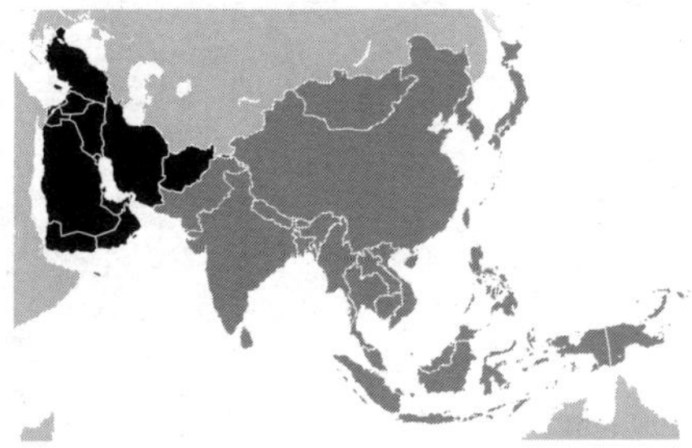

Words to Know

reservoir:
a place, such as a lake or pond, where water is gathered and kept for use as needed

Improvements in Farming

Farming has become more modern in some countries. In Turkey many farmers own their own land. Many of the village people in the mountains and coastal areas own a plot of land. Modern equipment has also been introduced to some of these countries. In the oil-rich countries such as Iran, Iraq, and the nations of the Arabian peninsula, the governments are using newly acquired wealth to improve farming and agriculture. Modern equipment, such as tractors and plows, is now used. In 1973 in Syria, a large dam was built. It created a huge **reservoir** called Lake Assad. Iraq is also building dams and reservoirs along the Tigris and Euphrates Rivers. These reservoirs will be used for irrigation, as well as for flood control and electric power. These dams will double the amount of land suitable for farming.

In Abu Dhabi, the capital of the United Arab Emirates, a new technique has been developed to improve farming. A layer of asphalt is being laid about three feet under a tract of sand. This stops irrigation water from sinking deep into the sand. It also prevents salt from seeping up from the subsoil.

Farming in Israel

Israel, like many other countries in the Middle East, is short of water and fertile land. In spite of these obstacles, more and more land is being made suitable for farming through the hard work of the new citizens of Israel. These Jewish people have come from many countries to settle in Israel. Many of them are skilled workers and have been educated in new farming technology. They have drained swamps, built dams, laid pipelines, built canals, and irrigated the desert lands. In southern Israel, which is mostly desert, farming has been very productive because of irrigation.

Many of the other farms in Israel are located along the coast, where the climate is pleasant and provides enough rainfall for farming. The main crops grown in Israel are olives, grapes, and citrus fruits, especially lemons and oranges. Some of these crops are grown in surplus and are exported to bring money into the country. Most of the meat eaten in Israel must be imported from other countries.

In some parts of Israel, the people band together to develop the land and to protect themselves from the nearby Arabs. They may live in small villages or on a *kibbutz*, a farm commune. A kibbutz is a farm owned and run by the people who live there. The people on a kibbutz are willing to work hard to start the crops. Sometimes they live with only the bare necessities until the kibbutz is well established.

LESSON REVIEW

Directions: Number your paper from 1 to 5. Then answer the following questions.

1. What types of irrigation are used in the desert areas of the Middle East?
2. What is a bazaar?
3. Describe improvements in farming that are taking place in some countries.
4. Which country is building reservoirs? How will they be used?
5. The kibbutz system has worked very well in Israel. Do you think this system would help to improve the economy of other countries? Why or why not?

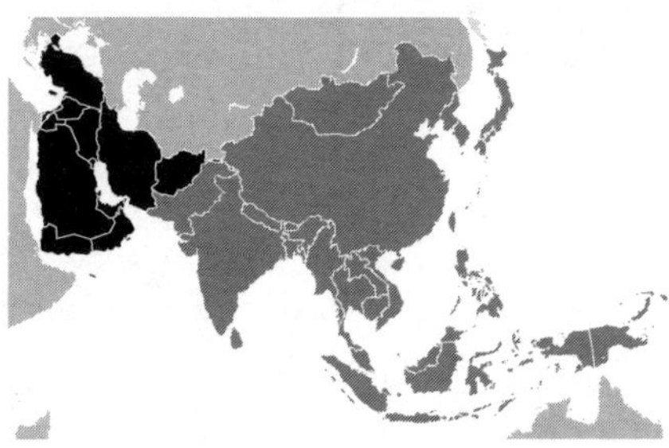

Words to Know

dictator:
a ruler who has complete power

sanitation:
developing and maintaining healthful conditions

LESSON 5: Life in the Cities of the Middle East

Cities have always been located along trade and water routes. In the past, cities were the centers for craftsmen and for farmers to sell their goods.

Today the cities of the Middle East are a mixture of the old and the new. Each city was built around a mosque, which is a Muslim place of worship. Cities were usually surrounded by a high wall for protection. These cities have sections with narrow streets and old buildings. New buildings, skyscrapers, modern schools, apartment houses with television antennas, and hospitals are built near these older sections. Automobiles, buses, and bicycles are replacing donkey carts in the city streets.

In oil-rich countries, such as Saudi Arabia, the cities are growing even more rapidly. These countries have money to build airports, roads, houses, office buildings, and shopping malls. Around the outside of the city are suburban areas where the workers live. Slum areas also house the thousands of people who cannot find work in the overcrowded cities.

Problems in the Cities

Many farmers and nomads are moving to the cities to find work. They are coming because their villages are too crowded or because they cannot support themselves by farming. Many of the cities do not have proper housing or enough jobs for these people. The people do not have the skills needed to work in the factories. In addition to unemployment, health care and education are also problems.

The governments of many Middle Eastern cities are working hard to solve the problems caused by the overcrowding of their cities. Housing projects are being built in some cities, and **sanitation** is being improved. Sewers, running water, and utility systems are being constructed. Health care and education have also been improved in many places. The governments are beginning to train the workers and managers in the skills needed to work in the factories.

The oil-rich countries—such as Iran, Saudi Arabia, and Kuwait—have been most successful in solving the problems of the cities. In the country of Kuwait the government has spent much of its wealth on education. Many wealthy countries, such as Saudi Arabia and Iran, are ruled by **dictators**, military leaders, or kings. These leaders decide how to use their country's wealth. In Iran a large amount of money was used to modernize the capital city of Tehran. The people of Iran complained because the villages were still very poor and lacked necessities such as running water.

Chapter 7 – Middle East

Ancient Cities

Some of the ancient cities of the Middle East have developed as the centers for trade, education, and government. Other cities in the oil-rich countries, such as Kuwait and Saudi Arabia, are new cities. They have been built since the countries gained their wealth.

Al Basrah, Iraq—Al Basrah is a seaport located where the Tigris and Euphrates Rivers meet. It is about 75 miles from the sea. In a famous story, the *Arabian Nights*, Sinbad the sailor sailed from Al Basrah. Most of the goods brought into Iran come through this port.

Beirut, Lebanon—Beirut, the capital of Lebanon, is home to about 25 percent of the country's population. Like all of Lebanon's important cities, it is located on the coastline. It is a large transportation center because of its road, air, and railroad connections and because of its seaport.

Baghdad, Iraq—This city can trace its history as a trading city back to ancient times. Merchants from the East brought their goods to Baghdad to sell. There are still many bazaars in Baghdad. Goods are sold on separate streets for shoemakers, tailors, metalworkers, and merchants who sell vegetables and fruits. The booths have colorful awnings. Visitors to Baghdad can also see caravans. A caravan is a group of merchants who travel across the desert and use camels or trucks to carry their goods.

Tehran, Iran—This city is the capital of Iran. When Iran became wealthy from the sale of oil, some money was spent on building skyscrapers and other modern buildings in Tehran. More than half of all the industry and business of Iran is centered in this city. Tehran is a mixture of the old and the new. For instance, women wearing *chadors*, or long, dark veils, can be seen walking down the modern streets of the city.

Damascus, Syria—This capital of Syria has been a trading city since ancient times. It is famous for textiles and ironworks. As in many Middle Eastern cities, there is an old section and a modern section. The older sections, where the bazaars are located, look much like they did in biblical times.

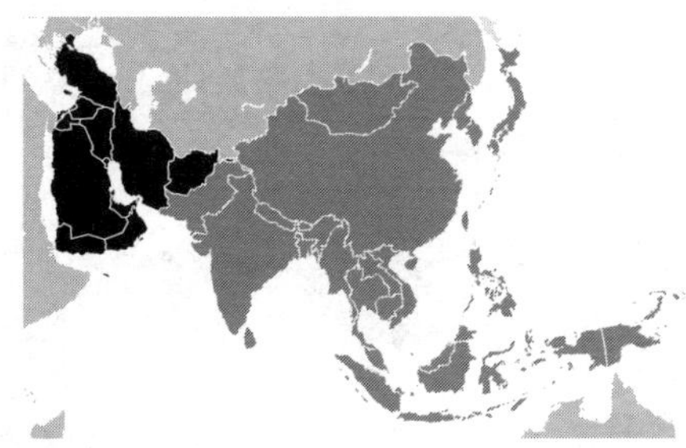

Words to Know

sheik:
an Arab chief

Mecca, Saudi Arabia—Mecca is the religious capital of the Muslims, and to them the holiest of all cities. Thousands of Muslim pilgrims come each year to visit the Great Mosque, which houses the Holy Kaaba. The *Kaaba* is a small stone building in the courtyard of the Great Mosque. It contains a sacred black stone to which all Muslims pray and hotels, expressways, tunnels, and parking garages have been built to take care of the pilgrims who come to the city each year.

Medina, Saudi Arabia—Medina is the second-holiest Muslim city and also has a large mosque. Medina has a university and famous library, where the holy book, the Koran, is kept.

LESSON REVIEW

Directions: Number your paper from 1 to 6. Then answer the following questions.

1. How were the early cities of the Middle East protected?
2. Name the cities that are well known for the following:
   (a) skyscrapers built with money earned by selling oil
   (b) textiles and iron works
   (c) the city of Sinbad in the *Arabian Nights*
   (d) many bazaars and merchants traveling in caravans
3. Why are Mecca and Medina important cities?
4. Many cities of the Middle East are a mixture of the old and new. What are some things you would see if you visited the older sections of the cities?
5. What are some similarities among the cities of the Middle East?
6. How are the problems of the cities being solved in some countries?

LESSON 6: Governments and Religion

Today, many independent countries in the Middle East have many different types of governments. Many of the Arab nations are ruled by kings, **sheiks**, or dictators. Jordan has a king who appoints a prime minister and a cabinet to rule. Saudi Arabia has a king who controls the entire government and is also the country's religious leader. This very religious country follows Muslim customs and traditions. Iraq and Syria are ruled by strong military dictators.

Two democratic countries exist in the Middle East. Turkey became a democracy in 1983. Officials there are elected by the people. The other democratic republic in the Middle East is Israel. It has a prime minister and a parliament, called the Knesset. The members of the Knesset are elected by popular vote.

Unrest in the Middle East

Most people in the Middle East want peace. For many years, since the creation of the nation of Israel, there has not been peace in this part of the world. Fighting began shortly after the United Nations declared Israel a nation in 1948. Then in 1956, 1967, and 1973, fighting between Israelis and Arabs broke out again.

Violence spread to areas called the West Bank and the Golan Heights in 1987. Many Palestinian leaders met several times to discuss peace and Palestinian self-rule.

Many Israelis and Palestinians agree that in the end Israel will give up land in exchange for peace. But years of fear, conflict, and distrust make progress toward peace difficult.

The discovery of oil has also caused unrest and conflict in the Middle East. Some countries that became rich from oil have not been able to manage their money wisely. Iran had many conflicts when the shah was overthrown. An ongoing civil war in Lebanon has taken place between Christians and Muslims.

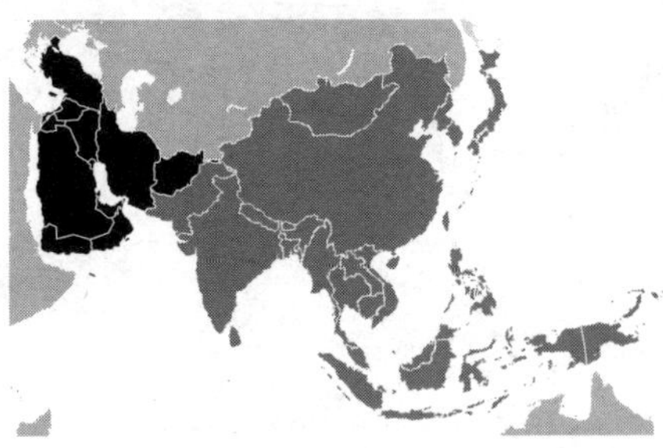

Words to Know

occupy:
to take or hold control of

The Persian Gulf War

Iran and Iraq are neighbors with a history of conflict. In 1988, a war with Iran left Iraq with a weakened economy. Then on August 2, 1990, Iraqi soldiers invaded Kuwait to take over its oil fields. The United Nations asked the invaders to withdraw, but they wouldn't. The United States then sent troops to Saudi Arabia to protect it and its oil from invasion by Iraq. This conflict became known as the Persian Gulf War.

During this operation, Iraq's leader, Saddam Hussein, set many oil wells on fire, causing great harm to humans, animals, and the environment. Efforts to resolve the problem peacefully failed, and the United States began bombing Iraq and the parts of Kuwait that Iraq had **occupied**. Allied troops entered Iraq and Kuwait, and several days later there was a cease-fire. The countries agreed that United Nations weapons inspectors would be able to inspect Iraq's stockpile of weapons.

Iraq repaired the bombing damage, but it still suffered from limits on oil sales and import privileges. Saddam Hussein kept his power and military strength. The weapons inspections have not gone well, and the area still suffers from unrest.

Chapter 7 – Middle East

Islam Is the Major Religion in the Middle East

Muslims, the followers of Islam, live in every country in the region. A few live in Israel. In countries like Saudi Arabia, 95 percent of the people are Muslims. The founder of the Muslim religion was Muhammad. He lived in the city of Mecca in Saudi Arabia. He believed that there was only one God, called Allah. Muhammad made the rules that are still followed by Muslims today: belief in one God, Allah; prayer five times a day; fasting (going without food) from sunrise to sunset during the holy month; helping the poor; and making a trip to the holy city of Mecca once during a lifetime. When Muslims pray, they must kneel, bow, and touch their forehead to the ground. Praying is always done while facing Mecca, the holy city.

After Muhammad's death, his followers put all his ideas in a book called the Koran. The Koran also tells the people how to lead their lives. According to the Koran, Muslims may not eat pork, drink liquor, or gamble. It also lists rules concerning marriage and divorce. The Koran is read aloud each Friday in a mosque, which is a temple of worship found in every Muslim city. Muslims are awakened each morning by a call to prayer from the mosque. On Fridays they are asked to make their noon prayers at a mosque.

These pilgrims are on their way to the Kaaba, the sacred shrine of Islam.

Mosques and Minarets

A mosque is found at the center of nearly every village, town, and city in the Arab world. Most are large rectangular buildings with a courtyard in the center. At one or two corners of the mosque are towers called minarets. Some are thin and straight, but others are spirals. The Muslim officials call people to prayer from the minaret. The mosque reminds the Arab of his Muslim religion and its values. Tall, modern buildings are now seen close to many mosques as the Middle East becomes more modern.

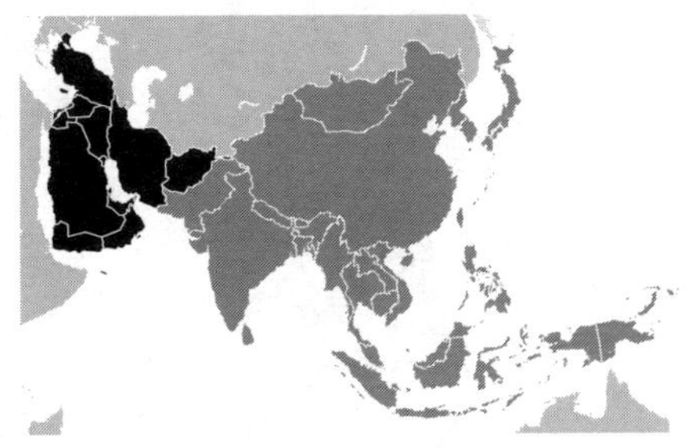

Words to Know

secluded:
to keep away from people or places

Customs, Traditions, and Family Life

The way many Middle Eastern people lead their lives is based on their religion. For example, in a traditional Muslim home, women are expected to lead **secluded** lives. A separate area called a harem is set aside for women. Only men of the family may enter the harem. Outside of the home, women wear veils and do not associate with strangers. The Koran says that men are to dominate women.

In the traditional Muslim family, the father rules his wife and children, and the family members are expected to obey him. If the father dies, his oldest brother or eldest son takes over. Among the nomads and some farm families, when the eldest son marries, he brings his wife to live in his father's house. In these families the daughters often have their husbands chosen for them by the family. Marriage is often a joining of two families for economic reasons.

In the cities women have a little more freedom. They may date, but they are strictly supervised. The parents still influence the choice of marriage partners. When a couple marries, they may live on their own. Housing is a problem in the cities, and it is not possible for a large extended family to live in the same apartment or small house.

LESSON REVIEW

Directions: Number your paper from 1 to 5. Then answer the following questions.

1. Who rules most of the Arab nations? Which Arab country's ruler is also the country's religious leader?
2. What are the two democratic countries in the Middle East?
3. What events have caused unrest in the Middle East?
4. What are some of the rules of Islam, the religion of most Middle Eastern people?
5. Do you think Muslim customs—such as the harem, wearing of the veil, and pilgrimages—will continue among the young people? Why or why not?

LESSON 7: Education and the Arts

In the past, in traditional Arab families, only boys received an education. They learned to do arithmetic and to write. They also became apprentices to shopkeepers or merchants. Some boys would be selected to go to special Muslim schools to learn the Koran. These boys became teachers, judges, or prayer-leaders in their villages and towns.

Today, in most Middle Eastern countries, the government provides an education for all citizens. Children go to public schools and learn reading, writing, history, and science. Illiteracy is still a problem in the Middle East, but it is decreasing as more and more children are attending school.

Literature

The three main languages of the Middle East—Arabic, Persian, and Turkish—have produced important poetry and prose. The *Koran* is the most important work of literature in the Arabic language. It contains the teachings of Islam. Poetry has always been popular among the Arabs, even before the Koran was written. Each ancient tribe had its own poet. The poet would write about warriors, customs, and the beauty of nature. The Persians, the ancestors of the present-day Iranians, also wrote beautiful poetry. The Persian poet best known in the English-speaking world is Omar Khayyam. He is well-known because his works were translated into English by a man named Edward Fitzgerald.

Stories and folk tales are enjoyed by all people. A famous story passed on by storytellers was *A Thousand and One Nights*, also known as *Arabian Nights*. By the nineteenth century short stories, novels, and essays were being recorded on paper. These literary forms were influenced by Western society.

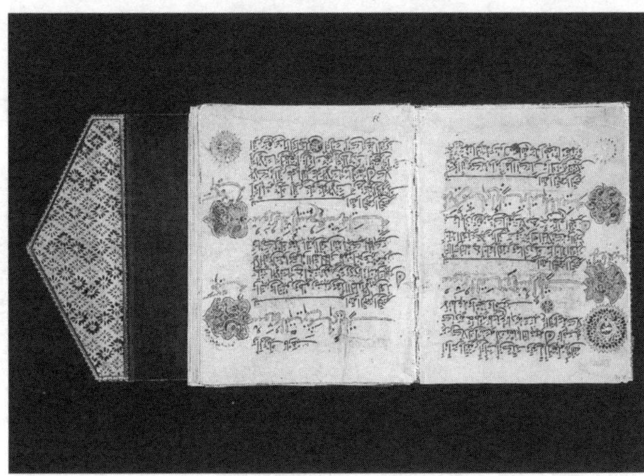

The Koran, the holy book of the Muslims, contains the teachings of Islam.

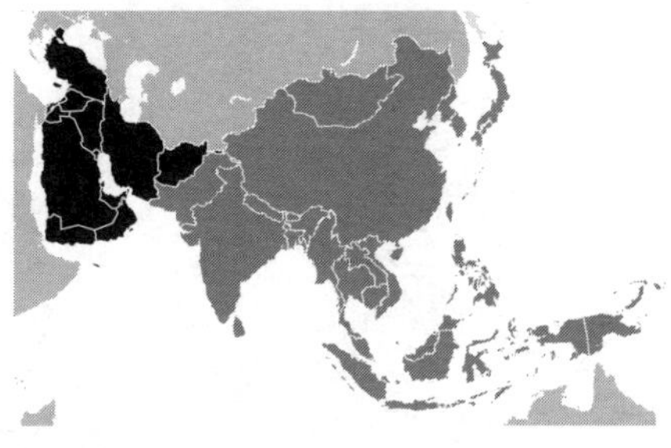

Fine Arts

Islam has had the greatest influence on art forms, especially architecture. The great mosques were built everywhere in the Middle East. One of the most beautiful is the Dome of the Rock in Jerusalem. Other art forms that developed were weaving, ceramics, pottery, and metalwork. The favorite way to decorate these works was with Arabic writing. Calligraphy, the art of elegant handwriting, became a major art form in the Muslim world.

The Muslim religion does not approve of music to accompany prayer. It also felt that paintings encourage idol worship; therefore mosques are decorated only with calligraphy and designs. As a result, music and painting developed only in the private courts and palaces of royalty.

LESSON REVIEW

Directions: Number your paper from 1 to 5. Then answer the following questions.

1. How is an education provided for most Middle Eastern children in modern times?
2. What is the holy book of the Muslims called?
3. What are some things not approved of by the Muslim religion? How did this affect the development of the arts?
4. Why do you think only boys received an education in traditional Arab families?
5. What did poets teach people about the ancient Middle Eastern tribes?

Spotlight Story

The Bedouins—Nomads of the Desert

The Bedouins are nomads found in the desert areas of the Middle East. The word *Bedouin* means "desert dweller." They have always been known for their good nature, hospitality, bravery, and kind treatment of strangers. They are wanderers who roam over the land in search of water and pasture land for their herds.

The Bedouins travel in large groups made up of family units. The leader of the group is called a sheikh. They move every few weeks in search of what they need. They live in tents and sleep and eat on rugs on the ground. When it is time to move on, they pack their belongings and leave. In the past, they used only camels to transport their goods. Today many Bedouins rely on trucks or jeeps. Trucks are also used to haul water to their herds. The camel is not as important as it once was; however, it is still used for milk and meat.

The life of the Bedouin is slowly changing. The number of nomads wandering with their herds is growing smaller each year. In the past they were rulers of the desert regions. They wandered where they pleased. Today, only a few groups remain as wanderers on the desert. Some have settled down near an oasis or other source of water. Many have become wealthy landowners. Other Bedouins have settled in the cities where they can get better health care, jobs, and education. Some Bedouins are not willing to give up their wandering life completely. They live part of the year near a settled area and spend the rest of the year in the desert.

SPOTLIGHT REVIEW

Answer the following questions.

1. What does the word *Bedouin* mean?
2. What is the leader of a Bedouin tribe called?
3. How did the Bedouins travel from place to place in the past? How do they travel today?
4. How is life changing for the Bedouins?
5. Why have some Bedouins settled near the cities?

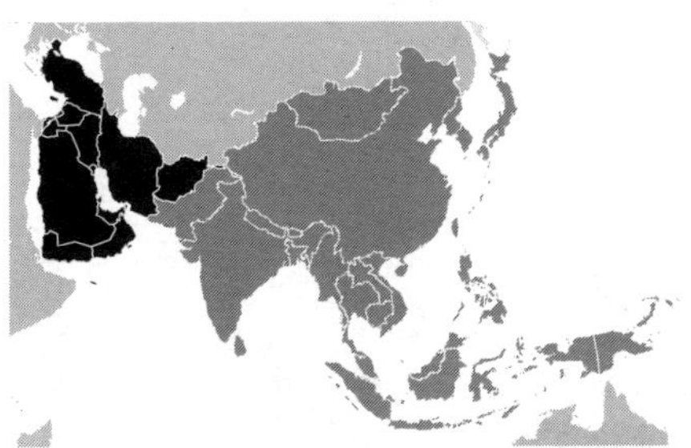

Chapter 7 Review

The lands of the Middle East are mostly desert, which makes the climate hot and dry. The moist areas are near the rivers, along the coasts, and especially near the Mediterranean Sea.

The history of the Middle East goes back thousands of years. Many invaders from other countries came and conquered the region. By the 1900s, most countries of the Middle East were free of foreign control. Today, most countries of the Middle East are ruled by dictators or kings.

The people of the Middle East are mostly Arabs. Islam, founded by Muhammad, is the main religion of the people. The architecture of the Middle East is evident in the mosques and temples. The Koran is the most famous work of literature to come out of this part of the world. Although most people in the Middle East want peace, progress toward that goal has been very slow.

These Turkish women are shopping in a busy marketplace.

Critical Thinking Skills

Directions: Give some thought to the questions below. Be sure to answer in complete sentences.

1. If you visited some of the oil-rich countries of the Middle East, what would you see in the cities and in the rural areas?
2. What are some of the steps Israel has taken to greatly improve its economy? Which of these do you think is most important?
3. Compare and contrast the lives of traditional Muslim women to most women of other religions in the United States.
4. In what ways has the oil economy of the Middle East changed the lives of the people?
5. How do you think the economy of the Middle East would have been affected if the Suez Canal had not been built?

For Discussion

1. How do you think the conflicts between the Arabs and the Israelis might be resolved?
2. In many countries of the world, women have taken on more and more important roles in society. Do you think this change will happen in certain countries of the Middle East? Why or why not?
3. Many countries of the Middle East are still developing. What are some of the ways in which they might develop in the future?
4. How might the government encourage the rural people to stay in the villages rather than to move to the overcrowded cities?
5. Of all the groups who developed in the Middle East through the years, which had the greatest influence on the present culture?

Write It!

Directions: Write a short paragraph. Describe how Bedouins lived for centuries and explain what is happening to them in modern times.

For You to Do

Directions: Find articles about business and industry in a Middle Eastern country and report the findings to the class. Many American companies have branches in some of the wealthy Middle Eastern countries such as Saudi Arabia and Kuwait.

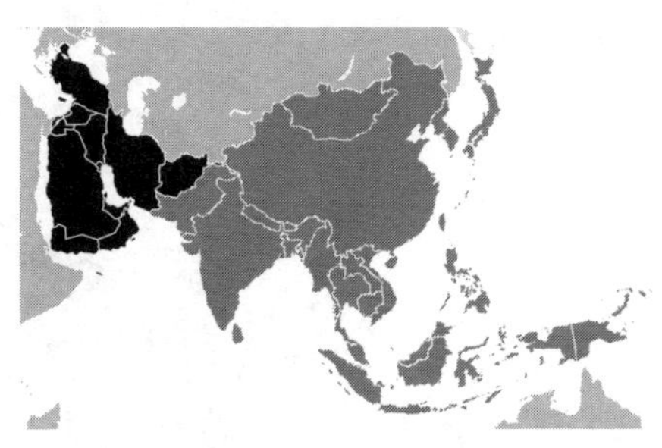

Glossary

acupuncture (ak´ yü pungk chər) an ancient Chinese practice of inserting needles into certain parts of the body to treat disease or relieve pain

ally (al´ ī) a person or a country who has a common plan or goal with another person or country

assassinate (ə sas´ n āt) to murder a famous person by secret attack

barren (bar´ ən) does not produce; has small amount or no vegetation

boycott (boi´ kot) to join together as a group and refuse to do or buy something

brocade (brō kād´) a type of cloth with woven designs

capitalist (kap´ ə tə list) a person whose money and property are used in business

caste (kast) a system of social classes dividing Hindus

Christianity (kris chē an´ ə tē) the religion based the belief in Jesus Christ and on the Old Testament and New Testament of the Bible as sacred scripture

civil war (siv´ əl wôr) a war between opposing groups of citizens of one nation

commune (kə myün´) a group of people living and working together; all property is owned by the group

Communist (kom´ yə nist) a person who supports communism, in which most property is owned by the state or government

complex (kom´ pleks) a group of related or connected buildings

constitutional (kon stə tü´ shə nəl) according to the constitution, or principles, of a nation

consumer (kən sü´ mər) a person who buys and uses food or products

contrast (kon´ trast) to compare differences

convert (kən vėrt) to change

cooperative (kō op´ ər ə tiv) an organization owned by and operated for the benefit of those using its services

corrupt (kə rupt´) dishonest; evil or wicked

delta (del´ tə) a deposit of soil, sand, and other materials at the mouth of a river

descent (di sent´) family line, ancestors

developing country (di vel´ ə ping kun´ trē) a country that is slowly developing its industry and economy

dialect (dī´ ə lekt) a certain form of a spoken language

dictator (dik´ tā tər) a ruler who has complete power

diplomatic relations (dip lə mat´ ik ri lā´ shəns) cooperation between countries that makes it possible to trade with each other

diverse (də vėrs´) different from something else; varied

dominate (dom´ ə nāt) rule or control

dowry (dou´ rē) money or property a woman brings to the man she marries.

dune (dün) a mound or ridge of loose sand heaped up by the wind

dynasty (dī´ nə stē) rulers belonging to the same family

economy (i kon´ ə mē) the system of making and trading things

enterprise (en´ tər prīz) a business organization

exile (eg´ zil) to remove or banish; separate from one's home or country

export (ek´ spôrt) to send goods to a foreign country

famine (fam´ ən) a food shortage that causes starvation

forebear (fôr´ bâr) ancestor

futon (fü´ ton) a quilt-like mattress placed on the floor and is used as a bed

harmony (här´ mə nē) in pleasant agreement

heritage (her´ ə tij) traditions inherited or passed down from one generation to the next

hibachi (hi bä´ chē) a grill that holds and burns charcoal for cooking or heating

illiterate (i lit´ ər it) not able to read or write; uneducated

imperialism (im pir´ ē ə li zəm) control or influence a powerful nation has over a weaker country

industry (in də strē) a branch of business or manufacturing

invasion (in vā´ zhən) an act of going beyond ones own boundaries or limits; usually to conquer or plunder another area

islet (ī´ lit) a little island

a	hat	e	let	ī	ice	ô	order	ů	put	sh	she	ə	a	in about
ā	age	ē	equal	o	hot	oi	oil	ü	rule	th	thin		e	in taken
ä	far	ėr	term	ō	open	ou	out	ch	child	ᴛʜ	then		i	in pencil
â	care	i	it	ȯ	saw	u	cup	ng	long	zh	measure		o	in lemon
													u	in circus

Glossary

isthmus (is´ məs) a narrow strip of land connecting two larger land areas

literate (lit´ ər it) able to read and write

massacre (mas´ ə kər) the cruel killing of large numbers of people or animals

merchant (mėr´ chənt) a person who buys and sells goods

minister (min´ ə stər) someone acting for someone else

minority (mə nôr´ ə tē) less than half of the whole part

missionary (mish´ ə ner ē) a person sent out by a church, to convert people to his/her religious beliefs

moat (mōt) a deep, wide ditch, often filled with water; may be found around a fortress or castle

moderate (mod´ ər it) not extreme

monsoon (mon sün´) an Asiatic wind that blows from the southwest bringing rains from June to October

natural resource (nach´ ər əl rē´ sôrs) a form of wealth produced by nature, such as water power, coal, and oil

nomad (nō´ mad) a person who wanders searching for food and/or pasture land

occupy (ä´ kyə pī) to take or hold control of

persecute (pėr´ sə kyüt) to treat cruelly or unfairly, often for reasons of religious or political beliefs

plantation (plan tā´ shən) a large farm that usually specializes in growing one crop, such as tobacco

prehistoric (prē hi stôr´ ik) describing a time before historical events were recorded or written down

prosper (pros´ pər) to be successful

reincarnation (rē in kär nā´ shən) a belief in the rebirth of the soul of a person into a new body or different form

reservoir (rez´ ər vwär) a place, such as a lake or pond where water is gathered and kept for use as needed

retaliate (ri tal´ ē āt) to pay back or get revenge

rickshaw (rik´ shȯ) a form of transportation in which a small two-wheeled carriage pulled by a man

ritual (rich´ ü əl) a ceremony that is performed as part of a special occasion, often as a religious

sampan (sam´ pan) a small, flat-bottomed boat

sanitation (san ə tā´ shən) developing and maintaining healthful conditions

secluded (si klü´ did) to keep away from people or places

shaman (shä´ mən) a person believed to have close contact with the spirit world; medicine man

sect (sekt) a group of people that believe in the same religious ideas

sheik (shēk) an Arab chief

slash and burn (slash´ ən bėrn) cutting down and burning trees to clear land, usually for farming

subsistence (səb sis´ təns) the production of just enough food to feed a farmers family

surplus (sėr´ pləs) an amount that is left over

technical (tek´ nə kəl) having to do with mechanical or industrial ability

technology (tek´ nolü ə jē) the use of science to do practical things

textile (tek´ stīl) a woven or knitted material

tradition (trə dish´ ən) something that has been handed down by generations that came before

typhoon (tī fo͞on´) a violent storm with winds up to 150 miles per hour

viceroy (vīs´ roi) person who rules a country or province, acting as the king or queen's representative

a	hat	e	let	ī	ice	ô	order	u̇	put	sh	she	ə { a	in about
ā	age	ē	equal	o	hot	oi	oil	ü	rule	th	thin	e	in taken
ä	far	ėr	term	ō	open	ou	out	ch	child	ᴛʜ	then	i	in pencil
â	care	i	it	ȯ	saw	u	cup	ng	long	zh	measure	o	in lemon
												u	in circus

Index

INDEX